Seeing Is Believing

Seeing Is Believing

An Introduction to Visual Communication

Arthur Asa Berger

Illustrated by the Author

Mayfield Publishing Company

Mountain View, California

Library of Congress Cataloging-in-Publication Data
Berger, Arthur Asa
  Seeing is believing.

  Bibliography: p.
  Includes index.
  1. Visual communication.   I.   Title.
P93.5.B445   1989   001.55'3   88–26627
ISBN 0–87484–873–3

Manufactured in the United States of America

10 9 8 7 6 5 4 3 2

Mayfield Publishing Company
1240 Villa Street
Mountain View, California 94041

Sponsoring editor, C. Lansing Hays; production editor, Linda Toy;
manuscript editor, Joan Pendleton; text and cover designer, Janet Bollow;
cover image, *Relief in Units,* © Vasarely (reproduced with permission).
The text was set in 10/12 Palatino by Progressive Typographers
and printed on 50# Finch Opaque by Malloy Lithographing.

Illustration credits appear on a continuation of the copyright page,
page 183.

Contents

Photography: The Captured Moment   61   Chapter 3

Film: The Moving Image 81

Television: The Ever-Changing Mosaic 97

Computers and Graphics: Wonders from the Image-Maker   157

Preface

The Audience

In recent years there has been a rapidly developing movement in our colleges and universities, especially in schools of communication and journalism, to do something about what can be described as the "visual illiteracy" of many of our students. It is possible, and quite likely often the case, that our students graduate without knowing very much (if anything at all) about how images communicate and people find meaning in them, about typefaces and graphic design, or about the difference between the film image and the television image.

Ironically, a significant number of our students hope to work in fields such as advertising, public relations, television, or journalism — fields where they will be involved, either directly or indirectly, with visual communication. Visual communication plays an important role in everyone's lives; we all watch television, we read newspapers and magazines and books, and we go to the movies. And we all live in an "information" society where much of the information we consider has a visual nature. It is important that everyone know something about how images function and how people learn to "read" or interpret images and various forms of visual communication. But it is particularly important that students in communication (and related areas) do so since those who create and use images have a responsibility to those who will be affected by them.

Mass Media Focus

One of the distinctive features of this book is that it focuses upon the mass media and deals with material of interest to students, material with which they are familiar. In this respect it differs from a number of books that deal primarily with visual communication as it relates to the fine arts.

Use of Semiological and Psychological Concepts

Seeing Is Believing uses semiotic and psychological concepts to help readers gain an understanding of how we find meaning in visual phenomena and how our minds process images. These concepts are presented in a readable manner, and numerous illustrations are offered to show how the principles discussed have been applied. These theoretical discussions are supplemented by a number of quotations from authorities that students will find useful and that will help them better understand the principles of semiotics and psychology.

Setting a Good Example

A great deal of attention was paid to the design of *Seeing Is Believing;* a book on visual communication should be attractive and show what good design is instead of merely talking about it. The book uses the power of graphic design and the visual image to facilitate learning. This book was designed by an award-winning graphic artist, Janet Bollow, after numerous discussions with the author. She also aided the author in finding some of the images, many of which are quite remarkable and all of which were chosen to illustrate, in a very direct and forceful manner, the topics discussed in the book.

Teachability

Seeing Is Believing was written to be a teachable book:

- It is written in an accessible style.
- It deals with topics that are of interest to students and that are part of their experience.

- It has arresting and remarkable images and visual materials to illustrate these topics.
- It is designed to be functional; that is, the book explains a number of concepts that readers can then use to interpret the images all around them. In addition, they are asked to use these concepts and ideas in interesting and creative ways.

Thus, at the end of each chapter, exercises and applications require readers to think about the textual material and then apply what they have learned in doing various projects, which they will frequently find entertaining.

A manual for teachers is available from the publisher; it contains a number of additional activities and exercises — to be used in the classroom or as assignments — as well as discussion questions and test questions.

The Style of the Book

Although the book deals with matters that are often complicated, the style of writing is, as has been suggested, readable. It might also be described as informal and perhaps even "breezy," though the latter term might be a bit extreme.

This style of writing was adopted consciously as a means of attracting the attention and maintaining the interest of the readers. The writing "sugar coats the didactic pill" as a means of enticing the students to deal with material that is occasionally technical and that they might otherwise try to avoid.

In other words, this book might not strike some as reading like a textbook; it also, to my way of thinking, is so attractively designed that it doesn't look like a textbook.

There is also a good deal of humor in *Seeing Is Believing*, another means of making it more attractive and less anxiety-provoking for its intended readers. (This may be a rationalization. The author is a humorist who, like many professors, sees himself as "really" being in training for becoming a stand-up comedian.)

If readers find this book entertaining, half the battle will have been won. And if there are a number of ideas as well as illustrations and images (by the author and others) that amuse readers and help humanize this text and make it more attractive to its readers, so much the better. The most important thing is to get students to read the book and learn something about visual communication.

Thanks

First of all I express my appreciation to my editor at Mayfield Publishing Company, Lansing Hays, whose ideas and suggestions played a major role in the way this book turned out. Every time I met with him it meant more work . . . and there were numerous meetings! But the book is much better as the result of his ideas and suggestions.

Equally important was the work of Janet Bollow, a fellow resident of Marin County (just north of San Francisco), with whom I spent endless hours discussing the design of the book and the images to be used in it. It is her fine work that has given form to my thoughts. Thanks also to Joan Pendleton for a superb job of copy editing the manuscript and to Linda Toy, my production editor.

Finally, let me express my appreciation to a number of people who read the book in its manuscript form and who offered many valuable suggestions, many of which I have adopted. They are Kevin G. Barnhurst, University of Illinois; Craig L. Denton, University of Utah; Sammye L. Johnson, Trinity University; Roy Paul Nelson, University of Oregon; Bill Ryan, University of Oregon; Linda Schamber, Syracuse University; and Birgit L. Wassmuth, University of Missouri Columbia. It is my hope that the work of all these people has led to publication of a book that will help students learn about the basic principles of visual communication and the role it plays in their lives and in society.

Seeing Is Believing

Image and Imagination   Introduction

Image

We live in a world of things seen, a world that is visual, and we expend much of our physical and emotional energy on the act of seeing. Like fish, we "swim" in a sea of images, and these images help shape our perceptions of the world and of ourselves. It is estimated, for example, that most of us receive more than 80 percent of our information through our eyes.

Images pervade our societies; we find them on billboards; in newspapers and magazines; on film screens and television screens; in our snapshots of children, friends, and relatives; in the paintings on our walls. These paintings, for example, both enrich our lives and convey to others something about our aesthetic sensibilities, socioeconomic class, and taste.

We communicate through images. Visual communication is a central aspect of our lives, and much of this communication is done indirectly, through symbolic means: by words and signs and symbols of all kinds. Our emotional states and our creative impulses need some kind of visual and symbolic expression to develop and maintain themselves, which explains why many organizations pay so much attention to visual phenomena such as costumes and uniforms, symbolic objects, signs, flags, and portraits and statues of important figures.

These images are needed to make philosophical abstractions or important figures from the past more real or concrete and to channel or focus our emotions more directly. It is very difficult to get emotionally involved with an abstraction, and so religious and political groups focus much attention on heroes, heroines,

I believe that one can learn to interrogate a picture in such a way as to intensify and prolong the pleasure it gives one; and if . . . art must do something more than give pleasure, then "knowing what one likes" will not get one very far. Art is not a lollipop, or even a glass of kümmel. The meaning of a great work of art, or the little of it that we can understand, must be related to our own life in such a way as to increase our energy of spirit. Looking at pictures requires active participation, and, in the early stages, a certain amount of discipline.

KENNETH CLARK, *Looking at Pictures*

great figures—who can be portrayed visually, with whom people can identify, and whose beliefs people can internalize.

Imagination

Imagination refers to the remarkable power our minds have to form a mental image of something unreal or not present and to use this power creatively—to invent new images and ideas. We can see a strong link between the terms *image* and *imagination*. Imagination exists in the mind, while the image—for our purposes—is tangible and visual. But the image is often a product of imagination, which means that the visible image is strongly connected to the mental one.

Creativity is defined in many different ways, and numerous theories try to explain what it is and why some people are creative and others are not (or don't seem to be). There seems to be a link between creativity and imagination—our ability to generate images in our minds, images *not* always representational or connected to anything in our experience.

Visual images help us discover things. In *Man and His Symbols,* the psychologist Carl G. Jung recounts the role dream images played in the discovery of benzene. Jung writes (1964:26):

> The 19th-century German chemist Kekule, researching into the molecular structure of benzene, dreamed of a snake with its tail in its mouth. [A representation of this from a third century B.C. Greek manuscript, is shown in Figure 0.1.] He interpreted the dream to mean that the structure was a closed carbon ring . . . [Figure 0.2].

This anecdote suggests that there is a strong link between visual images and what we call creativity. The images we see, whether in our dreams or daydreams, in drawings and doodles in our notebooks, or images we find in printed matter or films or the broadcast media—all are connected to our ability to focus our attention on something, to deal with it in other than abstract and intellectual ways, and ultimately to "break set" (escape from conventional ideas and beliefs) and come up with something new. If necessity is the mother of invention, the visual image is its father.

The Visual and the Psyche

Images have the power to reveal our mental states. Freud, in an early formulation, described the psyche as being divided into two parts, one accessible to our consciousness and one buried beneath our consciousness, an "unconscious." One might think

FIGURE 0.1
A rendering of a famous image—a snake with its tail in its mouth—found originally in a third-century B.C. Greek manuscript. The nineteenth-century chemist Kekule had a dream about a snake with its tail in its mouth, and this dream image led him to discover the molecular structure of benzene.

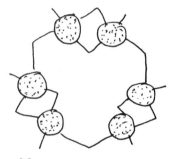

FIGURE 0.2
A rendering of the closed carbon ring that Kekule drew in his *Textbook of Organic Chemistry* (1861).

of an iceberg: the conscious element is the small part of the iceberg that is above the waves. Underneath is a huge mass, which we cannot see, that represents the unconscious.

Freud also explained, in a later refinement on his theories, that the psyche comprises three elements: the *id*, the *ego*, and the *superego*. The id represents drives, impulses, and sexual desire. The superego embodies moral beliefs (conscience) and ideal aspirations. The ego mediates between the two forces and involves the way individuals relate to their environment. The ego employs various defense mechanisms to achieve a balance between the forces of the id and superego. One of the most important of these defense mechanisms is sublimation, which involves the redirection of id energy from sexual matters to other areas, such as artistic expression. (Freud's theory is one explanation of artistic creativity.)

A number of years ago a German therapist, Anneliese Ude-Pestel, wrote *Betty: History and Art of a Child in Therapy*, a book about one of her patients — a little girl who was significantly disturbed (if not almost psychotic). Betty loved to make paintings and had made hundreds of them, which her father saved. The paintings were all ghastly — full of monsters and horrifying images, reflecting her psychological state. As the treatment progressed, Betty's paintings changed — and at the end of the therapy, when Betty had been restored to mental health, her paintings were those of a typical little girl (Figures 0.3, 0.4, 0.5).

The visual image, we see, has the capacity to show the anguish of a tormented soul just as it has the power to torment people, to

FIGURE 0.3
Betty's drawing, *Strangled Deadman*, drawn when she was six years old, before she started therapy.

FIGURE 0.4
Indian Girl on the Cross, drawn by Betty in the middle of her therapy.

FIGURE 0.5
Dancing Girl, by Betty. This picture was drawn by Betty near the end of her therapy and reflects her progress in overcoming her problems and becoming a normal little girl.

FIGURE 0.3

FIGURE 0.4

FIGURE 0.5

stimulate sexual desire, to generate intense feelings of patriotism and belief that often lead people to perform selfless acts of bravery or cruel acts of barbarism. It is not the image or symbol itself that is responsible but rather the ability of the image to call forth responses in people that are connected to their beliefs and values.

This power means, of course, that those who create images and symbols must think about the moral implications of what they do. Those individuals who, in some almost-magic way (which they may not completely understand themselves) have the ability to harness the power of the image must take responsibility for what they do. To the extent that seeing is believing, we must make sure that the images we create do not generate beliefs that are individually or socially destructive.

The Functions of Art

In his book *The Unchanging Arts: New Forms for the Traditional Functions of Art in Society*, the historian of art Alan Gowans suggests that the arts have always performed one (or more) of the following functions:

1. Substitute imagery
2. Illustration
3. Persuasion/conviction
4. Beautification

Gowans (1971:12,13) explains his theory as follows:

> Instead of asking "What is Art?" we need to ask "What kinds of things have been done by that activity traditionally called Art?" And then we will find that activity historically performed four functions: substitute imagery; illustration; conviction and persuasion; and beautification. (1) In cases where the appearance of something needed to be preserved for one reason or another, art made pictures that could be substituted for the actual thing. (2) Art made images or shapes (including pictographs) that could be used in whole or part to tell stories or record events vividly ("illustrate," "illuminate," "elucidate" all come from the same root "lux" = "light"). (3) Art made images which by association of shapes with ideas set forth the fundamental convictions or realized ideals of societies (usually in more ephemeral media). (4) Art beautified the world by pleasing the eye or gratifying the mind; what particular combination of forms, arrangements, colors, proportions or ornament accomplished this end in any given society depended, of course, on what kinds of illustration or conviction or persuasion a given society required its arts to provide.

Whenever we look at any work of art or any image (or visual field in general), we might consider what the "function" of the work is — as far as the viewer, the creator, society in general, and anyone else is concerned — and which of these four functions is dominant. We might also think about how an image is affected by the medium in which it is found and how a given work relates to other works. (Many works consciously borrow from other works — a phenomenon known as *intertextuality*.)

An Experiment

In the pages that follow this chapter you will find a number of images to examine (Figures 0.6–0.22). Instead of glancing at these images for the two or three seconds we ordinarily devote to such things (when flipping through a magazine, for instance), please study these works carefully. After you have examined them, please answer the following questions:

1. *What kinds of feelings did each of the works generate in you?* If you felt nothing, how come? If you felt strong emotions, how do you explain this? Did you, for example, experience envy, desire, anxiety, fear, repulsion, sadness, or joy? If so, why?
2. *To which element in your psyche* (id, ego, superego) *did each of the works primarily relate?* Why?
3. *Which of the four functions of art* (as explained by Alan Gowans) *dominated each image or work?* If you had trouble deciding the answer to this question, how do you explain that? Are there other functions that Gowans missed? If so, what are they?
4. *If you were asked to select a number of works to appear at the beginning of a book on visual communication, which works would you choose?* How would you explain your choice of each work? Would there be any unifying element to the collection of works? If so, what would it be?
5. *Do you find any unifying element in the works selected?* If so, what is it?
6. *If you were asked to make an exhibition of a number of works of art, images, or visual phenomena that expressed your personality, what would you choose?* If you had to choose ten images to represent America, which images would you choose?
7. *When was the last time you made a drawing or painting?* If you have not done one for a long time, how come? Why is it that when we are young children we love to draw, but when we get older, we generally give it up?

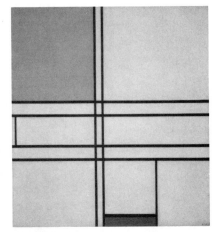

FIGURE 0.6
Mondrian, *Composition with Blue and Yellow*, 1935.

FIGURE 0.7
Ridley Scott, "1984" Macintosh commercial still, taken from television screen.

FIGURE 0.8
"Fidji" de Guy Laroche Perfume
advertisement.

"1984" by Thomas Porter, based on research by Robert Cook. This is a computer simulation of moving billiard balls.

Astronauts on the Moon.

FIGURE 0.11
Jason Berger, *Sketch of View from Graca,* 1978.

FIGURE 0.13
David Levine, *Lyndon Baines Johnson,* 1964.

FIGURE 0.12
Jason Berger, *View from Graca, 1978.* Oil
painting.

FIGURE 0.14
Antonio Frasconi, *Albert Einstein,* 1952.
Woodcut.

FIGURE 0.16
These two self-portraits show the difference between a rational and an emotional style of painting.

FIGURE 0.17
Joan Miró, *Woman and Little Girl in Front of the Sun*. 1946. Where is the woman? Where is the little girl? Where is the sun? Does this painting strike you as whimsical and amusing or foolish?

FIGURE 0.18
How do you explain the emotional impact
of this photograph?

FIGURE 0.19
Here are some interesting icons for you to examine. Would you say that functionality is the most important aspect of icons, or are design and aesthetic factors important as well?

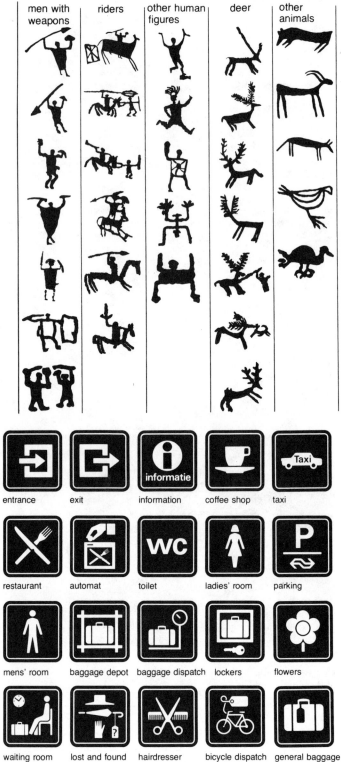

| men with weapons | riders | other human figures | deer | other animals |

entrance	exit	information	coffee shop	taxi
restaurant	automat	toilet	ladies' room	parking
mens' room	baggage depot	baggage dispatch	lockers	flowers
waiting room	lost and found	hairdresser	bicycle dispatch	general baggage

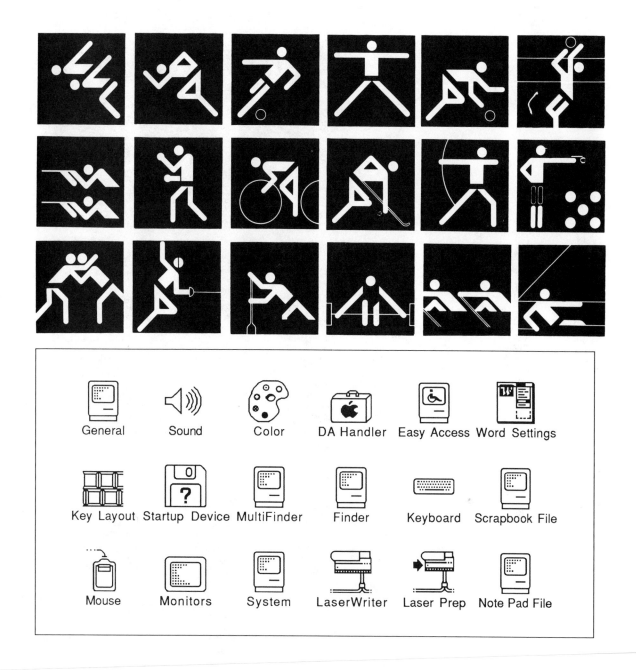

FIGURE 0.20
This illustration from *Grimm's Fairytales* is meant to generate the feeling of "horror" in people. What technique does the artist use to accomplish this?

FIGURE 0.22
Here is a still from a contemporary horror film. How does this still generate a feeling of horror?

FIGURE 0.21
Detail from Hieronymus Bosch.

Seeing Is Believing   Chapter 1

Seeing Is Believing

This book is called *Seeing Is Believing* because that phrase captures the essence of its argument—that visual phenomena, at
almost every moment, play an important role in our lives and
that our visual experiences are tied, directly and intimately, to
our intellectual and emotional ones. (In actual fact, seeing is *not*
or should not always be believing—because many things that
we "see" are false . . . or misleading or not real.)

Research suggests that many people are "obsessed"with their
looks—with their hair, their faces, their complexions, their
bodies, their arms and legs; and huge industries exist to help
people lose weight, conquer acne, get rid of "saddles" on their
hips or droopy eyelids—you name it. Surveys indicate that
though people claim they choose their spouses on the basis of
personality, religion, occupation, and other traits, in fact they are
initially attracted to them on the basis of looks.

We gain a great deal of information about others (and provide
a great deal of information about ourselves) on the basis of visual
matters. For example, think how important our cars are to us and
how important styling is for people when it comes to choosing a
car. For most of us, cars are not simply a means of transportation;
they are also, perhaps more importantly, statements about ourselves, our status, and our taste or style (Figure 1.1).

The same applies to our houses. People often judge us on the
basis of where we live, the size of our house, the style of our
house, and whether or not we have a view. The way a house is

*When we see, we are doing many things
at once. We are seeing an enormous field
peripherally. We are seeing in an
up-to-down, left-to-right movement. We
are imposing on what we are isolating in
our field of vision not only implied axes
to adjust balance but also a structural
map to chart and measure the action of
the compositional forces that are so vital
to content and, therefore, to message
input and output. All of this is happening
while at the same time we are decoding
all manner of symbols.*

DONIS A. DONDIS, *A Primer of Visual Literacy*

decorated—the color of the walls, the kind of furniture, the spatiality—all of these things might seem trivial and insignificant, but we know that they are connected to powerful and very deep aspects of our psyches.

People also evaluate us, perhaps unconsciously, on the basis of how attractive we are and how attractive our spouses are. Numerous surveys demonstrate that people judged ''attractive'' are generally more liked and come out rated higher in surveys than do people judged unattractive. We learn whether we are attractive or not by the responses of others. Our identities, then, are to a great degree fashioned by what have been called ''significant others'' via the feedback they give us about ourselves.

This also explains the anxiety people feel about ''blind'' dates. The term is important, for it directs our attention to the importance of the visual in our scheme of things. We might even have talked, on the telephone, to a so-called ''blind'' date; but because we have not seen this person, we generally feel uneasy. Numerous models and famous actresses tell tales of not having dates in high school or of having their mothers arrange for someone to

FIGURE 1.1
Notice the prominent role the automobile plays in this photograph by Bill Owens. Why do people feel so strongly about their automobiles? Why is it that our images are so dependent upon automobiles? Is it the automobiles themselves, or is it the advertising connected with automobiles that is significant here?

take them to the high school prom. The same applies for many famous men — statesmen, actors, and businessmen who were not exactly social lions when young. Not having a date on a given day means absolutely nothing.

The Visual and Personal Identity

We've already suggested that visual matters confer status on people — that others evaluate us on the basis of our cars and clothes and houses and spouses (Figure 1.2). The calculations these other people make generate ideas in their heads about who and what we are — about our identities.

And people refer to us, often, in terms of our physical attributes. Blondes supposedly "have more fun," and redheads are supposed to have tempers. Think also about baldness and the trauma it causes in men who often adopt bizarre hair styles in a futile attempt to hide their baldness. People are also described in terms of whether they are short or tall, thin or fat (or skinny or hulks), light or dark, and so on. Consider the role skin color has played in our history and in the history of many other nations.

Our physiques and other visible aspects can lead to nicknames that, it is likely, often play an important part in the way we develop our personalities. Undesirable identities probably lead to various kinds of compensating behaviors so that, to a certain degree, it might be argued that what we are or become is affected to a considerable extent by what we look like.

Seeing Isn't Believing

If visual matters are so important, it makes good sense for us to understand how visual communication works — the rules, principles, and codes that people use to interpret (or misinterpret) visual phenomena. *The principles discussed in this book can be applied anywhere — in magazine design, in newspaper layout, in advertising, in photography, in film and television making, or in something as humble as writing a resume — because these principles apply wherever visual matters are important, and they are important everywhere.*

We know, from watching magicians, that we can be misled by a visual phenomenon. Magicians don't saw people in half; they only seem to. We know, also, that people often have delusions, see "apparitions" that really aren't there, have dreams that are

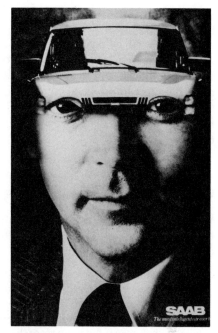

FIGURE 1.2
This is an extremely controversial Saab advertisement. The fusion of a face and a car creates a remarkably compelling image. In making this image, it was necessary to widen the distance between the eyes of the man so that they would appear in place of the headlights, giving him a curious (and, some suggest, idiotic) look.

"unreal," and are often fooled or misled by visual phenomena (Figures 1.3 and 1.4).

This book will help you learn how to interpret and understand visual phenomena more correctly and use them in a more reasoned manner. It will deal with principles of design and other matters involved in visual communication; with photography, film, television, typography, comics, and cartoons; and with the relationship that exists between visual matters and the imagination.

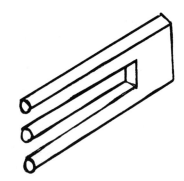

FIGURE 1.3
Optical illusion, "Devil's Tuning Fork."

Cognition and Visual Images

We actually expend a great deal of energy in the process of seeing things. In her book, *Understanding Video*, Jarice Hanson (1987:39) cites some fascinating statistics on this matter:

> It is estimated that 75 percent of the information entering the brain is from the eyes, and that 38 percent of the fibers entering or leaving the central nervous system are in the optic nerve. Current research indicates that the eyes have 100 million sensors in the retina, but only five million channels to the brain from the retina. This means that more information processing is actually done in the eye than in the brain, and even the eye filters out information . . .

Thus, we allocate much of our energy to processing visual information. We do this in the service of our cognitive faculties, or the means by which we acquire knowledge. This is generally done either through perception, intuition, or reasoning. For our purposes, the term *perception* will be used to deal with visual phenomena. We might, then, distinguish between *sight* or the ability to see, *seeing* or the actual process of using sight, and *perception* or the ability to apprehend and know the world by means of sight.

Robert E. Ornstein explains, in *The Psychology of Consciousness* (1972:27), that our eyes are always active:

> Our eyes are also constantly in motion, in large eye movements (saccades) as well as in eye tremors (nystagmus). We blink our eyes every second, move our eyes around, move our heads and bodies, and follow moving objects.

The term *saccades* is French and means "the flick of a sail." Each saccade takes about one-twentieth of a second—the same amount of time needed to make *persistence of vision* possible, the process that enables us to connect the frames of a film and "see" the film as continuous.

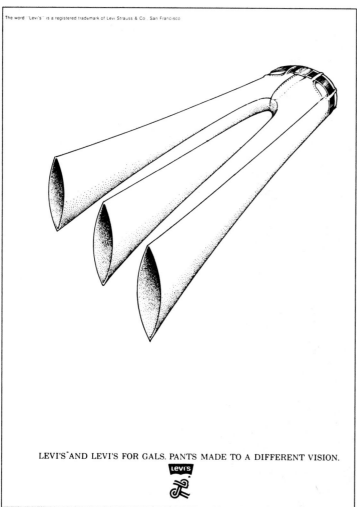

LEVI'S AND LEVI'S FOR GALS. PANTS MADE TO A DIFFERENT VISION.

FIGURE 1.4
Levi's advertisement based on the "Devil's Tuning Fork" optical illusion.

When we scan a fixed image, our vision fades after a few seconds, and we sweep it again and again to signal our brains to keep the image in our minds; when we follow a moving object, our eyes follow it and keep it fixed on our retinas (Figure 1.5). What we describe as vision is a physiological process that involves light striking our retinas and becoming registered by photoreceptors located at the back of the retinas behind blood vessels and nerve fibers. This information is then processed by the brain. Ornstein suggests that we have to fashion an awareness out of the different inputs we get (1972:27):

FIGURE 1.5
Scanning a "Nefertiti" postcard.

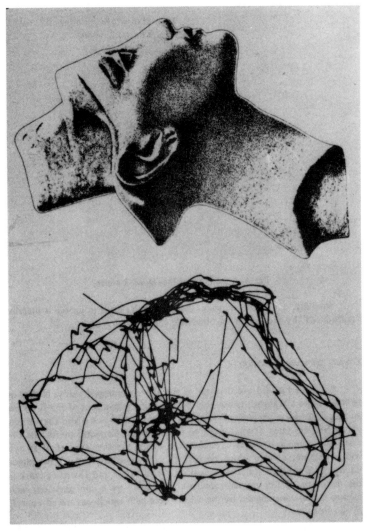

If we "saw" an "image" on our retina, the visual world would be different each second, sometimes one object, then another, sometimes a blur due to the eyes moving, sometimes darkness due to blinks. We must then construct a personal consciousness from the selected input, and in this way achieve some stability of awareness out of the rich and continuously changing flow of information reaching our receptors.

We must learn to select from all the information that is available to us and, in a sense, *construct* the world we see.

Our ability to process visual images seems to be related to our bicameral (two-hemisphered) brains. Research indicates that in normal people, even though both sides are involved in most activities, each hemisphere tends to specialize. Ornstein describes this phenemonon as follows (1972:51):

> The left hemisphere (connected to the right side of the body) is predominantly involved with analytic, logical thinking, especially in verbal and mathematical functions. Its mode of operation is primarily linear. This hemisphere seems to process information sequentially. . . . If the left hemisphere is specialized for analysis, the right hemisphere (again, remember, connected to the left side of the body) seems specialized for holistic mentation. This hemisphere is primarily responsible for our orientation in space, artistic endeavor, crafts, body image, recognition of faces.

As far as vision is concerned, both hemispheres of the brain play an important role.

Hanson (1987:41) tells us that while the left hemisphere is "more accurate in its ability to focus attention on something than is the right," the left side also tires more rapidly "and often gives way to the right." The right side maintains a general vigil in the surveillance of the environment, but it must call on the left hemisphere when it is necessary to pay attention to some detail.

When the right side does not call upon the left side, a process that might be described as image *narcotization* takes place—a sense of monotony and boredom. On the other hand, using the left side of the brain is tiring, and so it must be reserved for occasions when focus and detail are important. Thus both the left and right sides of the brain are needed, working in tandem, for people to process visual information in an optimal manner.

Aesthetics

Aesthetics means different things to different people. Courses in aesthetics, as it is conventionally understood, are generally given in philosophy departments and tend to be theoretical in nature. Philosophers typically deal with aesthetics in terms of the following abstract questions:

1. What is the nature of the beautiful? (Consider the Lachaise sculpture in this respect; see Figure 1.6.)
2. What is the relation that exists between form and content?
3. Is beauty objective or subjective? Does it exist independent of our opinions or is it mainly in the eye of the beholder, as some have suggested?

FIGURE 1.6
Gaston Lachaise, *Standing Woman (Heroic Woman)*, 1932, cast 1981. Does it make sense to ask whether you find this statue "beautiful," or is it better to ask how the artist achieved the effects he wanted to obtain in this work? What effects does this statue have on you? How did he attain the effects he wanted?

4.   What is the relationship between truth and beauty?
5.   What is the significance of ethical content? Need a work of art have moral value? If so, how do we define moral?
6.   What is the role of intention in evaluating a work?

These questions are important ones and ones that we might bear in mind as we proceed.

   This book, however, is about *applied* aesthetics and focuses upon the literal meaning of the term aesthetics, "space perception." The questions this book deals with are practical ones:

1. How do we obtain certain desired effects using the basic visual elements we have at our command?
2. How do we best exploit the powers (and deal with the limitations) of whatever medium we are working with?

In the world of applied aesthetics, we start with the *effect* we want and work backwards, using whatever we can to obtain that desired effect.

Taste is an important factor, of course, but it is very subjective. Taste is idiosyncratic; it is affected by matters such as sex, education, socioeconomic class, values, time, and culture. (Think, for example, how old-fashioned cars from the 1960s or fashions from just a few years back look today.) Some sociologists have suggested that there are "taste cultures" that shape the way people perceive things. From our perspective, that of applied aesthetics, taste reminds us that we must always know our audience and keep it in mind.

Conclusions

Seeing Is Believing aims to entertain you (in the best sense of term—namely, giving you ideas to "entertain") as well as teach you about visual communication, with the goal of helping you learn to see the world (and yourself as well) with more clarity and understanding.

Applications

1. List, in order of importance, the visual phenomena that are most important in shaping your identity. Consider such things as: height, body shape, hair color, hairstyle, complexion, teeth, eye color, clothes, etc.

2. List the most important status symbols in our culture. How do these symbols confer status on people? Is price the most important factor?

3. What makes a person "attractive"? Is beauty something that exists independent of people's opinion, or is it merely "in the eye of the beholder"?

4. It has been suggested that seeing isn't always believing—namely, that sometimes we are led astray by things we see. Give some examples of this. How can we use visual phenomena to deceive people?

5. In this discussion on aesthetics, a number of notions of what is most important in a work of art were mentioned: form, content, truthfulness, ethical qualities. Which of these concepts do you think is the critical one? What reasons can you offer to support your contention?

6. Aestheticians have suggested four theories of the purpose of art: (1) to generate emotional experiences in people, (2) to achieve certain consequences for individuals and society, (3) to mirror reality, and (4) to generate the artist's own reality. (These are known as the emotive, pragmatic, mimetic, and objective theories of art.) Which of them strikes you as best? Why?

7. What is taste? Is taste a valid and useful means of evaluating works of art and other phenomena? If so, why? If not, why not?

8. Select some advertisements from fashionable and upscale magazines such as *Vogue* and *Architectural Digest* and middle-scale magazines such as *Better Homes and Gardens*. What differences do you notice in terms of such matters as the physical features of the models (male and female) found in the advertisements? the way men are shown relating to women? how women are portrayed?

9. Draw a portrait of yourself in which you make yourself "better looking." What changes would you make in your features? Why?

10. Select some photographs or advertisements (with people in them) that reflect "beauty" in women and "handsomeness" in men. What do you find in common with selections made by your classmates? Have our definitions about beauty and handsomeness changed in recent years? If so, how do your photographs and advertisements reflect this?

Elements of Visual Communication

This chapter is an introduction to the elements of visual communication. It explains some of the most fundamental and important concepts that are needed to understand how visual communication functions. After reading this chapter you should have a much better knowledge of what has been described as "applied aesthetics," namely the way visual images and phenomena can be used, and have been used, to generate both emotional and physiological responses in people.

How We See

The first thing we must recognize is that we don't just "see" but have to learn *how* to see and *what* to see. We cannot focus our attention on everything around us; somehow we select certain things to look at. And what we decide to see is determined by what we know and what we believe and what we want. Consider our behavior in a supermarket, where we are surrounded by thousands of products, each clamoring for our attention. It is estimated we "see" eight products every second that we're in the supermarket. We may try to neglect the products we feel we do not need or want—but it is very difficult for most people to avoid purchasing some products on the basis of "impulse." (More than 60 percent of all supermarket purchases are not

Studies indicate that vision is about one-tenth physical and nine-tenths mental. In visual perception, sensory input in the form of light patterns received by the eye is transformed by the brain into meaningful images. The interpretation depends on preconditioning, intelligence, and the physical and emotional state of the viewer.

The variety of our responses to visual stimuli is demonstrated by artists. Twelve people depicting the same subject —even from the same vantage point— will create twelve different images because of their different experiences, attitudes, interests and eyesight.

DUANE AND SARAH PREBLE, *Artforms*

planned in advance, which means that impulse buying is a major factor in our trips to the supermarket.) And it is primarily as a result of packaging — that is, the way products look — that we are attracted to them. We are also affected by the design of supermarkets and the placement of products on the shelves. If we have to stoop down or reach up to get a product we are less likely to purchase it than if it is at eye level and easy to reach.

The way we think about visual phenomena is affected by our knowledge. In *Ways of Seeing,* John Berger points out that in the Middle Ages, when people believed in the existence of hell, fire had a meaning much different from and more powerful than its meaning today (Figure 2.1).

We all have to be taught what different objects are (a plane, a ship, a dog, and so on, ad infinitum), but we learn very quickly and with so little effort that we generally don't recognize that a learning experience has taken place. We just seem to pick up much of this information by osmosis — but the fact is that we do have to learn and that much of this learning involves visual phenomena.

There is a vast literature on visual matters — covering everything from highly abstract theoretical and philosophical treatises on the subject to reports on experimental research that has been carried out. And in between is a great deal of work that has been done of an applied nature, on such matters as how we perceive spaces, how we relate to colors, the responses generated by various kinds of film shots, the impact of editing, and the relation between a medium and its message, to cite just a number of topics.

We can't cover everything in this brief book, but by dealing with some of the most important aspects of visual communica-

FIGURE 2.1
Here are three renderings of fire. Our attitudes about fire are connected with everything from the myth of Prometheus (who stole fire from the gods and gave it to human beings) to our beliefs about the existence of hell.

tion, we can take that important first step on the "royal road" to visual understanding.

Signs, Symbols, and Semiotics

How do we make sense of the visual world? Many of us never bother to think about this question because we do a pretty good job of interpreting the world around us and rarely think about *how* we know *what* we know.

Consider the following:

- a drawing of a person (Figure 2.2)
- a house with smoke coming out of a window (Figure 2.3)
- a cross (Figure 2.4)

The list might go on endlessly: a photograph of a friend, a Rolls Royce, a flag, the Mona Lisa, the Eiffel Tower, the White House, the Pentagon, a Russian tank, a Big Mac, a computer, a giant white shark, the Washington Monument, the Leaning Tower of Pisa, a football, etc.

How do we "make sense" of these three items?

In Figure 2.2, the matter is quite simple: the drawing looks like the person; and so we can say that drawings (as well as photographs, paintings, sculptures, etc.) communicate by *resemblance*. In Figure 2.3, we know from our experiences with fires—in fireplaces, at ceremonial events, in television news shows or films—that "where there's smoke, there's fire." Thus we have good reason to believe that the smoke is *caused* by fire and that the building is on fire. In Figure 2.4, the cross is an object that we have *learned* is associated with Christianity and is an artifact having great resonance and emotional power for many Christians, since it symbolizes Christ's crucifixion. There is no way for a person to "naturally" know the meaning of a cross; there is no logical connection between the object and what it stands for the way there was between smoke and fire. (The connection is historical, not logical.)

Now let us consider another matter related to visual communication that we might add to the preceding list:

- the word *tree*

The word *tree* and the object it refers to are shown in Figures 2.5 and 2.6. Linguists tell us that there is no natural connection between a word and the object it stands for. Thus, the word *tree* and the object it stands for (defined in Merriam-Webster's *Ninth New Collegiate Dictionary* as a "woody perennial plant having a

FIGURE 2.2
Here is a very simple drawing of a man.

FIGURE 2.3
A house on fire. "Where there's smoke, there's fire."

FIGURE 2.4
A cross.

single, usually elongate main stem generally with few or no branches on the lower part") are not logically related. *The relationship between a word and the object it stands for is arbitrary or conventional.* This fact explains why dictionaries need to be revised all the time, since language is always changing. This same relationship between a word and its object also applies to all kinds of other phenomena, in which we learn that something (a word, a facial expression, an object, a hairstyle, etc.) signifies or stands for something else.

Let's recapitulate. We make sense of visual phenomena in a number of ways:

1. *Resemblance* (as in photographs)
2. *Cause and effect* or logic (as in smoke implying fire)
3. *Convention* (as found in objects that have symbolic value)
4. *Signification* (as in a smile signifying pleasure)

There is a science which is of great utility in helping us understand how visual phenomena communicate—a field of knowledge called semiotics, the science of signs. Two theories are encompassed here: one is the field known as semiotics, which was developed by the American philosopher C. S. Peirce, and the other is the field known as semiology, developed by the Swiss linguist Ferdinand de Saussure. For the sake of simplicity, we'll use the term *semiotics* to cover both of these theories.

A sign, from the semiotic perspective, is anything that stands for something else. What does this statement mean? Only that a great deal of communication is done not directly but rather indirectly, by using various signs. For instance, there are several ways to suggest that an actor is portraying a secret agent (Figure 2.7). The actor could say "I am a secret agent," or a narrator could tell us. Or the actor could wear a trench coat and a slouch hat, carry a small revolver with a silencer, and drive a fast sports car. All of these matters are signs that—taken together—suggest a secret agent.

Peirce identifies three kinds of signs: iconic, indexical, and symbolic, as the following chart shows. An icon is a sign that looks like or resembles the thing it stands for—which means that icons are easy to interpret; the drawing in Figure 2.2 is an icon. Because icons are so easy to interpret, signs in airports are often icons—pictures that most people, regardless of the language they speak, should be able to understand. An indexical sign is logically connected to what it represents; in Figure 2.3 smoke indicates fire. We have to learn about this connection and do so, often, just from everyday life. A symbol, on the other hand, has conventional meaning, and there is no logical connec-

FIGURE 2.5
The word *tree.*

FIGURE 2.6
Drawing of a tree.

FIGURE 2.7
Ways to suggest a secret agent.

tion between this meaning and the symbol itself. It is something we have to learn, as in Figure 2.4.

	Icon	Index	Symbol
Signify by	Resemblance	Causal connection	Convention
Examples	Photograph	Smoke/fire	Cross Flags
Process	Can recognize	Can figure out	Must learn

Peirce's theory is actually very involved, but these three concepts at its center are of great use to us in understanding visual communication. For example, internists and other "cognitive" physicians (in contrast to surgeons and others who are "operative" ones) work on the basis of indexical knowledge. They see various signs and patients tell them about their symptoms; and on the basis of these phenomena, they try to determine what is causing a problem. All of us recognize the power of symbols on people — flags, the crucifix, the Star of David, college banners, logos . . . one could go on endlessly. These symbols often generate enormously powerful emotional responses in people. In fact, people are often willing to give their lives for the institutions and organizations behind these symbols.

Peirce said that "the universe is perfused with signs, if not made up entirely of them," which means that *everything can be seen as a sign of something else* and that human beings are sign-producing and sign-analyzing beings (Figure 2.8 and 2.9). If everything in the universe is a sign or can be understood as one, it certainly makes sense to learn how to interpret and understand signs.

FIGURE 2.8
Logos for Saturn motorcars. The four versions of the Saturn logo are the final ones produced. Logo (A) was chosen. All offer somewhat different "images" for the automobile, and all contain pictorial references to the planet Saturn.

FIGURE 2.9
Logos for Black & Decker show how the company has modified its image over the years and reflects how aesthetic values have evolved over four decades.

The second theory, Saussure's, argues that a sign is divided into two parts: a signifier and a signified. A signifier is defined by Saussure as a sound or object that calls to mind a concept or *signified*. This can be represented by Figures 2.10 and 2.11. According to Saussure, the relationship that exists between the signifier and signified is arbitrary or conventional—that is, the relationship must be learned and is not natural.

Therefore, in Saussure's view, no signifier—whether a word or a drawing or any other kind of sign—is self-explanatory and implies a specific signified. A specific facial expression—a wink, for example—can mean a number of different things, depending upon the situation. As the semiotic theorists often point out, if signs can be used to tell the truth, they can also be used to lie.

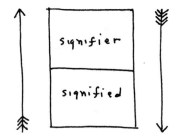

FIGURE 2.10
Signifier/signified diagram.

What Signs Can Do

Let's look at several examples of how signs can mean different things and how we can use them for a variety of purposes. For one thing, we can lie with signs. People who dye their hair are, from this perspective, "lying" with signs—though this kind of lying is not considered of great consequence. People who lease expensive cars and present themselves as owning them are, in a sense, lying with signs (or, in this case, status symbols). When we laugh at a joke that we have heard before so that we don't embarrass the joke teller, we are lying. Or are we merely being polite?

FIGURE 2.11
Signifier/signified diagram for *tree*.

No sign, when some kind of a sign is expected, is also a kind of sign. If you say hello to a friend and don't get a response, that is a sign. Not doing something when something is expected of you is a kind of sign for a behavior known as "aggressive passivity"; in other words, doing nothing or not responding can, in certain situations, be seen as a form of aggressive behavior. This "aggressive passivity" or "passive aggression" is often used by children to "get back" at their parents—for example, children "take forever" to do their chores.

Signs are used by people as a means of getting information and coming to conclusions about things. During the Iran-Contra hearings of 1987 commentators made much of the participants' facial expressions and body language—as a means of trying to understand what the participants *really* felt or believed. In the case of William Casey, the late CIA director, however, this was impossible, because Casey was "stone faced" (Figure 2.12). Furthermore, the president, Ronald Reagan, had a long background in acting, and actors are people who can pretend to have feelings and beliefs that they don't really have.

FIGURE 2.12
These photographs show two faces—one
of William Casey that gives very little
information about his feelings and
emotional state and one of James Dean that
is very expressive and gives a great deal of
information.

Codes

Since the relationship that exists between signs and what they
mean (from Saussure's perspective) is arbitrary, we have to find
ways of making sense of signs; we do so via codes. Codes can be
looked at as ways of making sense of signs, as systems of conventions that we are taught or pick up from our culture. In fact, what
we know as culture, in the anthropological perspective, can be
looked upon as a collection of codes.

In some cases, these codes are created and systematized—as
in the driving codes that we all must learn in order to get a
driver's license. These codes are collections of rules that tell us
what to do when we see certain signs and when we find ourselves in particular situations. Thus, we learn that when we see a
red light we must stop our cars and when we see a green one we
can start our cars or continue on if we have not stopped.

These codes list the conventions we have adopted in order to
make it possible for us to drive and get from one place to another
with the minimum of danger and confusion. Figure 2.13 shows
some of the visual signs and symbols used on roads and high-
ways. Some of these signs are iconic, and we can make sense of
them without having to be taught what they mean; but others
are symbolic and conventional. We must learn what they mean.
In some cases we have redundancy, in which a message is repeated in several ways to reinforce its impact.

FIGURE 2.13
Highway signs use icons or language, and sometimes both, to convey their messages. Note the simplicity of the drawings in the icons.

These driving codes and others like them are one kind of code. They are really collections of laws and rules. There are other kinds of codes, however, that are learned more or less by osmosis as people grow up in a particular culture. These involve the whole universe of beliefs (many of which exist at a level below awareness or articulation) that tell us what things mean or what to do in given situations.

We have certain ideas about what being a "blonde" means, about what having a weak chin means, about what having "shifty" eyes means, about what being short or tall or fat or skinny means. We have notions about what certain kinds of food mean and when to eat salad, for instance. In the United States we eat salad before the main course while in France and other European countries, the salad is generally eaten after the main course. (What we call culture shock is generally the result of finding oneself in a society where the codes or culture-codes are different from the ones we are used to.) We have notions of how to dress for interviews and what certain styles, colors, and fashions mean. We should recognize here that it is also possible to misinterpret signs. Because of differences in education, region, class, and so on, people often interpret (or *decode,* to use the semiotic term) signs in widely varying ways. This aberrant decoding is a problem for people—such as writers, artists, film makers, and especially those who make commercials and print advertisements—who try to convey something to people but find them interpreting it in unanticipated ways.

Many of these codes are connected to visual matters, as we've already suggested. And much of what we know or think we know from observing various visual signs is based on associations we make or have been taught to make about signs and what they signify. The technical term for these associations is *metonymy.* An example of this phenomenon would be an advertisement for Scotch that shows the liquor being used by people who live in a mansion and are obviously rich and—it is suggested— have good taste. We learn to associate that brand of Scotch with what might be called "high class" people and upscale living. The advertisement in Figure 2.14 is an example of the use of metonymy or association. Advertising makes great use of the power of *association* since this technique conveys information quickly and powerfully.

Another important method of transmitting meaning involves using *analogies*—saying or suggesting that something is like or similar to something else. Consider the two statements that follow:

1. My love *is* a red rose.
2. My love *is like* a red rose.

In the first case we are making a very strong kind of analogy and are, in fact, suggesting equivalence. This figure of speech is known as a metaphor. In the second case we are suggesting that our love is similar to a red rose, a figure of speech known as a simile. In both cases, the meaning is created by making an analogy. Some scholars argue that metaphor is the basic way we have of knowing about the world and that human thinking is essentially metaphoric.

Metaphor and simile are not confined to words and written language—they also are part of visual language and pervade our image making (Figure 2.15).

"I was wondering if I could possibly borrow a cup of Johnnie Walker Black Label."

12 YEAR OLD BLENDED SCOTCH WHISKY. 86.8 PROOF. BOTTLED IN SCOTLAND. IMPORTED BY SOMERSET IMPORTERS, LTD., N.Y., N.Y.

FIGURE 2.14
Johnnie Walker advertisement. This advertisement uses the association
(metonymy) of wealth and elegance to suggest sophistication and quality.

It is not unusual for a given sign or symbol to have both metonymic and metaphoric aspects to it; that is, to communicate by using both associations and analogies.

Think, for example, of our old friend, the snake. We, in the West, *associate* the snake with Adam and Eve in the Garden of Eden and with our eating from the Tree of Knowledge and being expelled from Eden. So the snake is connected, in Western minds familiar with the Old Testament, with deception ("The serpent beguiled me," Eve says) and a host of other negative things like having to work and having to die. On the other hand, snakes are long and thin (which means their shape makes them resemble penises) and thus they are *analogous* to or also function as phallic symbols. (In certain Asian countries, on the other hand, the fact that snakes shed their skins and become "new" again leads people to associate snakes with rebirth and immortality.)

Quite obviously, it is very difficult to communicate anything with precision and certainty, since signs are so open to interpretation and misinterpretation and convey their information in so many different ways.

FIGURE 2.15
Here is a visual metaphor that you might find amusing.

Condensation and Displacement

To further complicate matters, we must understand something about how the mind processes signs and symbols and other visual phenomena. Think of your dreams, for instance. In your dreams you see all kinds of fantastic things. Sometimes you see several different things tied together in bizarre ways. You might see a train with wings or a building floating in water. In dreams, the mind, for its own reasons, unifies disparate phenomena and creates fantastic images (Figure 2.16).

The Bible is full of remarkable dreams and visions which feature incredible images and about which there is still much controversy. Consider, for example, the famous vision of the prophet Ezekiel:

> And I looked, and behold, a whirlwind came out of the north, a great cloud, and a fire infolding itself, and a brightness was about it, and out of the midst thereof as the color of amber, out of the midst of the fire. Also out of the midst thereof came the likeness of four living creatures. And this was their appearance; they had the likeness of man. And every one had four faces, and every one had four wings. And their feet were straight feet; and the sole of their feet was like the sole of a calf's foot; and they sparkled like the color of burnished brass. And they had the hands of a man under their wings on their four sides . . . As for the likeness of their faces, the four had the face

FIGURE 2.16
Ezekiel and the whirlwind. Ezekiel's vision
remains a puzzle to this day. Some have
suggested that what he saw was a visit by
aliens to the earth; others believed he was
deranged and was "seeing things."

of a man, and the face of a lion, on the right side, and the four had had the face of an ox on the left side; the four also had the face of an eagle.

The process by which we combine elements of various signs together to form a new composite sign or symbol is called condensation. There is another process of importance called displacement. In this process we transfer meaning from one sign or symbol to another so that a rifle or a plane really stands for a phallus, if you understand what is going on and know how to interpret such matters.

These terms come to us from Freud, who discussed them in his classic book, *The Interpretation of Dreams*. He used the terms to explain how the psyche uses images to evade what he termed the dream censor and avoid being wakened. By condensing images or displacing content from one image to something else, we "trick" the dream censor, so to speak. In many cases, these condensations and displacements involve sexual matters. These two techniques enable us, then, to have our sexual fantasies and, by disguising them and fooling the dream censor, to avoid being wakened.

These terms are important because much of what we find in visual phenomena involves the use of these processes and, as in dreams, much of visual communication takes place at the unconscious level. And these processes also are connected to profoundly important unconscious matters in our psyches, which explains why so many visual phenomena have the emotional impact that they do. Symbols carry a great deal of emotional baggage, both on a cultural level and on a personal level and have the power to evoke powerful and often unrecognized responses in us.

What Freud has described as phallic symbols—rifles, umbrellas, knives, and other objects similar to a phallus in shape and function—are really good examples of displacements. Our society does not allow us to show male and female genitalia in print advertisements, for example, but it is possible (and often done, many argue) to use phallic symbols that evade the censors and call to mind various aspects of our sexuality. Consider here the symbolic significance of the monument for George Washington, the father of our country, being a large phallic shaft stretching up into the sky (Figure 2.17).

Surrealistic styles, which unite all kinds of disparate phenomena, are examples of condensation in action (Figure 2.18). And the power of surrealistic styles (found often on MTV) stems from the psychological associations connected with the various signs and symbols pulled together.

FIGURE 2.17
Washington Monument.

Signs, Symbols, and Semiotics | **37**

As the various paintings, advertisements, and other works reproduced in this book show, we generally find signs existing in some kind of context that includes other signs and symbols. This combination of signs and symbols is what we commonly describe as an image.

FIGURE 2.18
Surrealistic image, by Bob Malecki.

The Image

From our perspective, *an image is a collection of signs and symbols* —what we find when we look at a photograph, a film still, a shot of a television screen, a print advertisement, or just about anything.

According to *Webster's Ninth Collegiate Dictionary* an image is ''a tangible or visible representation.'' The word can also be used to mean a number of other things, including a mental representation we have of something, such as "the image of the business-man in nineteenth-century American literature."

Images are visual, generally speaking, often mediated—carried by the mass media—and they are connected to information, values, beliefs, attitudes, and ideas people have. This connection is not a natural one, remember; we have to learn to interpret many signs and symbols, which are important component elements of images. An image is a collection of signs, and each of these signs has meaning; in any image there are many different levels of meaning and interactions between meanings.

Think of an advertisement where a man is shown smiling and drinking a stein of frosty beer in a tavern; from his facial expression, he seems to be having a good time. In this image (which may be accompanied by words), the bubbles in the beer, the frost on the stein, the foam, and the smile all are signs meant to convey information and generate certain attitudes in the minds of those who look at the advertisement.

Images, of course, do not come into existence of their own volition. They are generally created and mediated, meant to be seen and read, and to have a specific function and impact. Let us now consider how images relate to media, creators, audiences, and society in general. We can focus on images in regards to

the artists who create images

the audience, which receives images

the work of art, which is an image itself and might comprise a number of images

the society in which the images are found

the medium, which affects the images

A complex interaction of these five factors makes the way images work difficult to describe. The artists or creators of the images try to use signs that the audience will interpret or decode correctly; in this case, "correctly" means the way the artists want them to. The image itself is affected by the medium in which it is found, by various artistic conventions, in a given medium (for example television is often held to be a medium dependent on "close-ups" due to the small screen) and by the audience to which the image is directed. Signs and symbols such as Uncle Sam or the Republican Elephant also often have historical significance that may be recognized by some people and not by others. These signs may allude to important cultural, political, historical, and social experiences that a stranger in the society might not recognize or understand (Figure 2.19). Because of all these complications, communicating anything clearly and unambiguously is difficult. These factors also make our communications powerful and even put them beyond the control of those who create signs and symbols. It might be suggested that often communication takes place between the unconscious of the creators — the artists — and the unconscious of the receivers — the audience — so that the situation becomes even more mixed up. Nobody, in such a situation, completely understands or fully appreciates what is being communicated and what impact it is having.

FIGURE 2.19
Jan Van Eyck, *Giovanni Arnolfini and His Bride*, 1434. Many of the symbols used in this painting were understood in Van Eyck's time but are not generally recognized now. Thus, the lighted candle in the chandelier signifies Christ's presence and the ardor of the newlyweds as well; the convex mirror suggests the eye of God seeing everything and seems to reflect the painter and another witness; the dog symbolized marital faithfulness; the bride has her hand on her stomach (and appears to be pregnant), signifying her willingness to have children; the fruit is tied to symbolism connected with the Virgin Mary; the carving in the back of the chair is of St. Margaret, the patron saint of childbirth; and the shoes are probably an allusion to the commandment by God to Moses to take off his shoes when on sacred soil. The signature of the painting and the date are also prominent, to record this event. When looking at a painting or any image of a symbolic nature, what we know determines how fully we can understand and interpret it.

One thing is certain—images do have powerful emotional effects on people. Your self-image, for example, affects the perceptions others have of you; and their perceptions, in turn, affect the image you have of yourself. It is not unusual for people to change their images over the years and create new "identities" for themselves, as they move through their life cycles and find themselves in new situations. A person might be a hippie in his twenties, wear three-piece suits and be a "buttoned-down" businessman in his forties, and become a priest or rabbi in his sixties—three major changes in identity (and "look") in one lifetime.

Images often have a historical significance. The meaning a given image has may also change over time, as a society develops and changes its views about things. Images also play an important role in religion and the arts. Think of the importance of visual elements in our religious ceremonies, in which we find people performing certain ritual activities, wearing certain costumes, using certain artifacts, and doing so in a space full of signs and symbols. The lighting is often important in such ceremonies for it helps generate specific attitudes—such as a feeling of awe or piety or mystery.

To see how the various aspects of images work, examine the following chart, which summarizes much of the discussion made to this point.

DECODING VISUAL COMMUNICATION

Concept	Example	Method
Icon	Photograph	Resemblance
Index	Smoke from window	Cause and effect
Symbol	Crucifix	Convention
Signifier and signified	Bowler Hat = Englishness	Convention
Condensation	Face/automobile	Unification
Displacement	Rifle = penis	Substitution
Metaphor	Spiderman's costume	Analogy
Metonymy	Huge mansion = wealth	Association

Elements of Analysis of the Visual

In the material that follows we deal with some of the most important elements found in visual fields. We start with the dot, which can be looked upon as the most fundamental element in all visual communication—the element from which everything else is built.

The Dot

The first element in analyzing the visual is a dot, a small circular point in space. Dots can be used to indicate a shape, as Figure 2.20 shows.

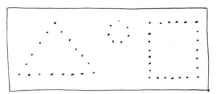

FIGURE 2.20
Dots.

The Line

A succession of these dots or points where the individual dots are not distinguishable forms a line, one of the basic elements found in visual phenomena. We use lines to indicate what things look like and what their shape is like. Lines are sometimes formed on their own, by drawing them, but they are also formed as the edge of shapes.

Different artists develop differing kinds of lines; we can see this variation in the work of cartoonists. Some have a smooth, liquid, delicate line and others have a heavy, rough kind of line. Lines can have their own qualities and generate all kinds of responses.

The Shape

Lines can be generated, more or less indirectly, from shapes; but they also can create shapes—in outline form. According to Donis A. Dondis, in *A Primer of Visual Literacy*, there are three basic shapes: the *triangle* (an object made from three lines), the *square* (an object made from four lines of equal length at right angles to one another), and a *circle* (a figure in which all points in the circumference are equidistant from the center point) (Figure 2.21). All other shapes or figures can be thought of as being variations on these three basic shapes. Dondis suggests that these three basic shapes have their own character. She writes (1973:44):

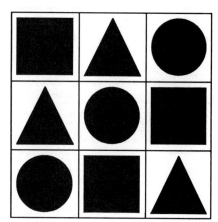

FIGURE 2.21
Triangle, square, and circle. These shapes are the basic elements or fundamental building blocks found in all visual communication. They are simple, elegant, and powerful.

> Each of the basic shapes has its own unique character and character-istics and to each is attached a great deal of meaning, some through association, some through arbitrary attached meaning, and some through our own psychological and physiological perceptions. The square has associated to it dullness, honesty, straightness, and work-manlike meaning; the triangle, action, conflict, tension; the circle, endlessness, warmth, protection.

Shapes, then, by themselves, have the power to create certain feelings and responses.

In some cases, shapes are created by forming lines; but in other cases, shapes are formed as the result of other phenomena. Think, for example, of the figure-ground relationship and the famous problem it presents to our minds (Figure 2.22). It is a drawing of two faces in profile *or* of a vase, depending upon how we look at it. What is important to recognize is that it is impossible to see *both* the profiles and the vase at the same time. We can see either the vase or the profiles, either the figure or the ground.

This figure-ground concept is important in other cases, for we often find that the ground helps determine the meaning of a figure, in the same way that the context in which a word is found often helps us understand how the word is meant to be understood (Figure 2.23).

Volume

If we think of shape as a two-dimensional figure (length and width), then when we move into a third dimension — depth — we get an object, something that has volume. Our eyes are used to a world where objects have volume, and most of the visual phenomena we are involved with have volume — or seem to. A drawing of a building is a two-dimensional figure that tricks the eye into thinking it is seeing something in three dimensions (Figure 2.24).

FIGURE 2.22
Figure and ground representation. One can see either the faces or the vase, but not both together at the same time.

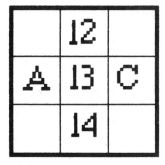

FIGURE 2.23
This figure shows the importance of context in interpreting visual phenomena. Many images are somewhat ambiguous and depend upon the context in which they are found for meaning. Read down, the image in the center block is a number, 13; read across, it is the letter B. Thus a syringe can suggest drug dependence or medicine, depending upon whether the syringe is seen in a "shooting gallery" or a hospital.

FIGURE 2.24
This drawing suggests volume by adding depth to the dimensions of length and width.

ANT   HUMAN   HUMAN   MOUNTAIN

FIGURE 2.25
Scale. Scale is a concept based on some kind of a comparison. Thus a human being is gigantic relative to an ant and insignificant relative to a mountain.

Scale

Scale refers to relations in size between shapes and objects. Unless we have a scale of reference, we cannot know how large or small something is just by seeing it. If, for example, we see a drawing of a human figure, we immediately can set the scale, since people tend to be between five and six feet tall (Figure 2.25).

Semiotics tells us, in fact, that concepts have no meaning in themselves; they make sense only because they have some relationship to some other concept (most often their opposite). In the same way, shapes and objects are indeterminate in size until placed into a relationship with some other shape or object whose size is known.

Scale carries emotional impact. The feelings we have when we are in a small room are different from those we have when we are in a gigantic space where we are "dwarfed" and seem insignificant.

Spatiality

Our discussion of scale leads to the matter of spatiality, an important element in pictorial design. We have learned to associate large spaces with wealth and class and small spaces with the opposite; perhaps this association comes from the houses, mansions and estates in which the wealthy live. So the way space is used in a composition tells us something and generates specific responses. In this respect, consider the difference between an advertisement for groceries, as found in any newspaper, and an advertisement for an expensive product, as found in any upscale magazine. There is no white or empty space in the typical supermarket ad, which is crammed with lists of items and how much they cost. In the upscale product advertisement, on the other hand, there is often a great deal of white space (Figures 2.26 and 2.27).

Our attitudes or feelings about what space means are quite likely based on associations and are metonymic. White space becomes associated with upper-class or upscale products and life-style, and so we learn to "read" the use of white space in a

FIGURE 2.26
Detail from supermarket advertisement. The supermarket advertisement attempts to convey as much information about as many products as it can and thus tends to be full of lists and very crowded.

The Romance
of
Waterford

Gump's collection

of hand-cut Irish crystal

ranges from biscuit barrels,

paperweights and clocks

to jam jars, scent

bottles, vases and bowls.

From 37.50

Valentine's Day February 14th.

GUMP'S
SINCE 1861

Wilshire at Camden   Beverly Hills   (213) 278-3200
Valet Parking

FIGURE 2.27
Advertisement for Gumps. Advertisements for upscale stores tend to be
simple and have a great deal of "white" or "empty" space.

certain way. This reading is a coding we learn; as we grow up we learn many codes that help us make sense of the advertisements and other visual phenomena to which we are exposed.

Balance

There are essentially two kinds of balance: axial or formal balance and informal balance. Formal balance has the elements of the composition arranged equally on both sides of imaginary axes in the composition. This design is very formal and static. With informal or asymmetrical balance, the situation is different; there is no desire to have balance — in fact, imbalance is deliberate, and asymmetry generates stress, energy, and visual excitement.

We generally use the term *composition* to describe the way line, shape, volume, scale, and balance are used in a visual work, whether it be a painting or photograph or advertisement. Just as there are certain rules for writing words in the correct manner (what we call grammar and syntax), there are also rules for assembling elements in a visual work.

Figures 2.28 and 2.29 demonstrate the two approaches to balance. Notice how formal and static the advertisement with the axial balance is, how it lacks dynamics, or movement. We associate this kind of balance with antiquity, formality, sophistication, and elegance; products that desire to generate this kind of impression often use axial balance. In the same manner, products that wish to convey a different feeling (and this includes most products) don't, as a rule, use axial balance. If you examine Figures 2.28 and 2.29, you will notice that they convey different impressions, in part through their use of balance.

Direction

Lines and shapes direct our eyes to move in certain directions. When we look at an image, our eyes tend to start in the upper left corner and then move around the image as we are directed to by lines, shapes, and other phenomena.

Herbert Zettl uses the term *vector* for direction and shows how powerful vectors are in all the visual media. He defines a vector as a "force with a direction and a magnitude" (1973:386) and suggests that we must use the notion of vector fields in order to understand film and television, which present us with moving images.

In advertising, direction is often used to focus attention on certain kinds of information (textual, pictorial) that is of central

© 1987 See's Candy Shops, Inc.

FOR THE 66TH YEAR IN A ROW,
WE WON'T MAKE THE BEST DRESSED LIST.

But for the 66th year in a row, we at See's
will make the best chocolates list. And the reason is simple...
We make the best chocolates.

Caramel   Almond Cluster   Bordeaux   **See's.**   Chocolate Butter   Cocoanut Cream   California Brittle

FAMOUS OLD TIME CANDIES.

FIGURE 2.28
Advertisement for Mrs. See's Candies. This advertisement is very formal and
uses axial balance to suggest restraint and quality. It has very little text and is orga-
nized in a symmetrical manner around imaginary vertical and horizontal axes.

One of the best ways to lose weight may be to eat more fiber.

That's because foods with a lot of dietary fiber, like the California prune, provide roughage. So you feel full. And fiber foods smooth out the absorption of nutrients, which may help reduce hunger between meals. In other words, with a balanced diet—less fat, more fiber, moderation, and a variety of foods—you'll be well on your way to a trimmer you.

And few foods are a better choice for fiber than prunes. They're one of the richest sources of fiber—with 9 grams per serving. Prunes are also a good source of Vitamin A and potassium. With no fat, no cholesterol, and almost no sodium.

One way to serve your family prunes is baked into a muffin. You'll find more helpful serving suggestions in our free brochure. For your copy, write to Prune Ideas, P.O. Box 882168, San Francisco, CA 94188-2168.

Besides, while prunes are a spoonful of natural sweetness, each prune has just 25 calories. Dieting never tasted so good.

Prunes. The high fiber fruit.

© California Prune Board 1987

FIGURE 2.29
Prunes advertisement for California Prune Board. This advertisement is an example of dynamic balance, which is used to suggest informality.

importance. Our eyes are "led" to the copy and then to an image. An advertisement may exist in two dimensions and be just a moment in time; but by using vectors for directing our eyes, it is possible to give a kind of life to the advertisement, as we move throughout it. We look at different parts of it and read all kinds of different meanings in it. We do the same for paintings and photographs and most visual phenomena.

Lighting

The kind of light we find in an image is extremely important. Our ability to see anything is a function of light; at night, as the saying goes, all cats are gray. Light can be used to direct the eyes.

And lighting shapes our perceptions of things — it shows us what things look like by illuminating shape, texture, and color and by manipulating shadows to generate certain feelings and attitudes. Lighting is one of the tools the artist and photographer can control and is an extremely powerful aesthetic device.

There are two basic kinds of lighting: flat lighting, in which the differences between light and shadow are more or less minimized, and chiaroscuro (kee-are-oh-skuro) lighting, in which the differences between light and shadow are emphasized (Figures 2.30, 2.31, and 2.32). Flat lighting reaches its extreme in hospital operating rooms where shadows are, to the extent it is possible, eliminated. Chiaroscuro (in Italian its two parts mean "clear" and "obscure"), with its strong lights and shadows, is associated with works of intense emotion: photographs of the dead and horror films, for instance. The following chart lists the differences as they generally exist:

Flat	Chiaroscuro
strong light, weak shadows	strong lights and shadows
rationality, knowledge	emotion very powerful
soap opera	tragedy, horror film, etc.
operating room	graveyard

Naturally, lighting exists in all degrees of strength or intensity, depending upon the purpose being served; and a given kind of lighting can be used in many different ways.

The French semiotician, Roland Barthes, has recognized the power of lighting. In *Mythologies* (1957:15) he discusses professional wrestling and suggests, in his chapter on "The World of Wrestling" that:

The virtue of all-in wrestling is that it is the spectacle of excess. Here we find a grandiloquence which must have been that of ancient

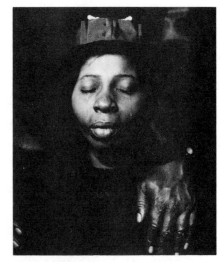

FIGURE 2.30
Chiaroscuro lighting. This photograph has very strong lights and darks, giving it a dramatic quality.

FIGURE 2.31
Flat lighting. This photograph has even or flat lighting. It reveals more than the one with chiaroscuro lighting but has less impact.

theatres. And in fact wrestling is an open-air spectacle, for what makes the circus or the arena what they are is not the sky . . . it is the drenching and vertical quality of the flood of light. Even hidden in the most squalid Parisian halls, wrestling partakes of the nature of the great solar spectacles, Greek drama and bullfights: in both, a light without shadow generates an emotion without reserve.

What Barthes points out is that *it is the nature of the lighting which establishes, in essence, the intensity of the experience for people.* Other examples might be our association of a kind of lighting with the holy; think of cathedrals and their shafts of light.

FIGURE 2.32
Arnold Newman, *Martha Graham,* 1961. This photograph is an excellent example of flat lighting. It was printed in a manner that emphasizes the difference between Graham and the stark and flat walls of her dance studio. © Arnold Newman.

Color

Color is an enigma. It is generated by electromagnetic waves; various wavelengths or combinations of wavelengths reflected off an object send messages to our eyes that we then interpret as a given color or colors. When we see an object that reflects back most of the light that falls on it, we see it as white. When we see an object that absorbs most of the light that falls on it, we see it as black. Consider the following attributes of color:

1. *Hue.* This is the color itself. Example: red, yellow, etc. The primary hues are red, yellow, and blue.
2. *Saturation.* This is the strength or purity of the color. Example: light blue, deep blue, etc.
3. *Brightness.* This refers to the lightness or darkness (or tonal gradations) of an image. It is not tied to color itself but to the intensity of light generated by an object. Thus, a given screen image (or still) shown on a color television set and a black-and-white television set will have the same brightness.
4. *Warmth and coolness.* We describe certain colors—red, orange, and yellow—as warm and others—blue and green—as cool. By mixing elements of cool colors into warm colors, we can cool them down (or by adding elements of warm colors to other warm colors, warm them up). Colors that are opposite one another (such as red and green, orange and blue, or yellow and purple) are known as complementary colors. When mixed together they produce gray.
5. *Contextual relationships.* Colors are affected by other colors near them. A given color can be made to seem weaker or stronger depending on the color it is placed next to. If a circle of bright yellow is placed in a square of gray it looks different than it will if placed in a square of red.

There is a good deal of debate among scholars about whether the way we respond to various colors is natural or cultural. Why, for example, do we use red for stoplights and stop signs on our roads? Why do green lights mean "go"—other than the fact that we say they do in our rule books? Some scholars have argued that red has a particular significance to us because it is the color of our blood, and so our attitudes to red are, at least to some degree, natural. (This view is questioned by many other scholars.) Whatever the case, experience shows that colors have a profound physiological and emotional impact on people.

This explains why people are generally very careful about the color of the clothes they wear when they are interviewing for jobs. In the old westerns, the villains often could be identified by the color of their clothes (black); the heroes, naturally, wore white (for innocence?). Now many organizations engage color consultants to determine the right color schemes to motivate workers and make people feel good about their surroundings. Hospitals and many other institutions have found that color plays an important role and has a profound effect upon people. Color also is a significant aspect of cuisine; the way foods look and the colors that are combined are carefully chosen in French,

Californian, and various upscale cuisines. This is because colors give "messages" to which we respond.

Interestingly enough, the messages colors have vary from culture to culture. In some cultures black is associated with death while in others white is associated with death. So our responses to color are, it seems, some kind of a combination of natural and culturally conditioned ones.

We see the world in color (unless we are color-blind), which means that black-and-white photographs and films, now that we have color photography and film, have increasingly taken on status as "art"—something distant from our everyday reality. There is a great deal of controversy now over the practice of "colorizing" old black-and-white films and television shows. The people who own the film rights want to color them to attract larger audiences, but many directors and producers find the practice a violation of artistic integrity; black-and-white film was the medium for creation of the image and therefore part of it.

Perspective

As strange as it might seem, what we call linear perspective is a relatively recent development in the arts; the ancient and early medieval painters did not know how to create the illusion of depth or of three dimensions on a two-dimensional plane, which explains why their work seems so flat—though it is often quite beautiful. Perspective was, one might say, "discovered" during the Renaissance (Figures 2.33 and 2.34). Perspective involves

FIGURE 2.33
This photo makes excellent use of the Z-axis, in which the road leads vertically from the viewer toward infinity.

representing things the way they look, with parallel lines converging on some point (imaginary or real) on the horizon line via the process of psychological closure.

Psychological closure refers to the way our minds "complete" incomplete visual material that is given to us (Figure 2.35). We fill in the blanks, so to speak. We also form a gestalt or "whole" out of bits and pieces of information that we have—unifying them into something that is more than the sum of the parts. This process works everytime we watch television, as Zettl explains (1973:137):

> The low-density (possessing relatively small amount of visual information due to the limited number of scanning lines) television picture relies quite heavily on our facility for psychological closure. Although our persistence of vision ("seeing" something for a short period after it has already been removed from our vision) helps us to perceive the scanning dot of the TV image as a complete image, we need to apply psychological closure to relate the low-information patterns on the screen into meaningful visual images.

The process which also is at work when we look at photographs with halftones, is automatic and not dependent upon our wills or intentions.

Look at Figure 2.36. Notice how the lawn and the sky (given direction by the trees) converge on the horizon line, where we find the mansion. This is an excellent example of one-point perspective, in which our eye is led to one point (the vanishing point) that exists on the horizon line. (There is also two-point perspective, in which we sometimes don't see the second point but can infer or imagine it from looking at the work; see Figure 2.37.) This vanishing point is the focal point of Figure 2.36; and

FIGURE 2.34
This work, created during the Renaissance, shows that artists during this period had become masters of perspective.

FIGURE 2.35
This drawing leaves a great deal of information out and relies on the eye and previous experiences we have had for "closure."

You can tell from the outside
which Scotch they serve on the inside.

Johnnie Walker®
Black Label Scotch
YEARS 12 OLD

12 YEAR OLD BLENDED SCOTCH WHISKY, 86.8 PROOF. BOTTLED IN SCOTLAND. IMPORTED BY SOMERSET IMPORTERS, LTD., N.Y. © 1981

FIGURE 2.36
Johnnie Walker advertisement. This image shows the power of perspective as
our eye is led from the huge and elegant gate to the mansion at the horizon
line. Note how the lawn and the trees converge on the mansion, an excellent
example of one-point perspective.

FIGURE 2.37
This shot, taken from below, shows the power of perspective.

just under it, highlighted by color, we find a message in white and a Johnnie Walker sign in yellow. These two elements are outside the massive gate, which signifies power, through its size, and taste, through its delicate and beautiful ironwork.

Now examine a work that does not make use of perspective, Angelo Puccinelli's *Tobit Blessing His Son,* the work of a four-teenth-century Italian painter (Figure 2.38). Unlike modern paintings, in this painting objects distant from us are not reduced in size. This does not mean that works created before the mastery

of perspective are inferior; many of these works are exquisite, but they are products of a different aesthetic system.

The placement of a horizon line generates a certain sense of spatiality (or lack of it) that has emotional consequences. The horizon line we see in the far western United States, which stretches out before us endlessly, suggests for most people an immensity and grandeur that we feel is somehow ennobling. Not being able to discern a horizon line often has the opposite effect; it can make us feel trapped and uneasy.

Proportion

Proportion involves the relationships of elements in an image or some other visual phenomena. One of the most famous "laws" of proportion is that of Pythagoras who is supposed to have discovered "the golden section." This law states that in a line, for example, the relationship of a small segment to a large segment should be the same as the relationship of the large segment to the entire line:

(X   (Y)   Z)
YZ is to XY as XY is to XZ

This relationship is found all through visual phenomena—in paintings, in architecture, in advertisements—because the eye finds it naturally pleasing.

When you deal with proportion, the following factors should be considered:

Size: large/small
Shape: regular/irregular; dense/scattered
Axis: vertical/horizontal
Color: dark/light; warm/cold; bright/dull

All of these factors play a role in the way we create and respond to visual images.

Conclusions

Marshall McLuhan, the Canadian communications theorist, argued that "the medium is the message." He meant that a medium (such as television or radio) was more important than the content (the various programs, commercials, announcements, etc.) it carried. This position is obviously extreme—but McLuhan was correct in calling our attention to the power of the media—and, relative to our concerns, visual images—which many people tend to neglect.

As we can see from this primer in applied aesthetics, an image (such as those we see in a magazine advertisement or on our television screen) is an extremely complex phenomenon. Matters such as line, shape, dimension, lighting, design, spatiality, color, and perspective all can be looked at as conveying "messages" or being kinds of sign information that have an impact upon us. Sometimes we are aware of this impact; but sometimes the message goes to our unconscious where, it can be argued, the message might have profound effects upon us. (The "messages" we get from artists and writers often move from their unconscious to ours; they don't know the full extent of what they are doing and we don't know the full extent of how we are being affected.) Anyone who has ever seen an advertisement for a product and experienced a strong desire to purchase it knows that visual phenomena are powerful and can excite us. Artists, writers, and other creative people can, as they say, "push our buttons."

This chapter was written to illuminate some of the basic elements found in visual communication; knowing about these elements might help us understand the ways in which we can be stimulated and excited and have our buttons "pushed." In the chapters to follow, you will see that these elements keep appearing and reappearing, for they are the building blocks from which all visual phenomena are constructed.

Applications

1. Applying your knowledge of semiotics, assume you are a television director and wish to give your viewers information and elicit certain feelings without using words. What visual phenomena — that is, what images — would you show on the screen to generate the following concepts: horror, terror, secret agent, "Frenchness," love, hate, alienation? Choose some other concepts. Remember, also, that sometimes the combination of visuals generates the concept.

2. Bring any small, simple object that you think reflects or signifies your personality to class in a brown sandwich bag and give it to your instructor. (This is to prevent people from knowing who brought what.) Write your name on the bottom of the bag and list the attributes the object has that you expect your classmates to find. Does the class interpret the object correctly, or do they see things in it that surprise you? What do you learn from this exercise?

3. Analyze a full-page, color advertisement that has people in it in terms of the signs found in it. (Remember that words are signs also.) What signs do you find? How do they work? Do you detect any codes functioning? If so, what are they, and how do they work?

4. Write down a dream you had in as much detail as you can. Then use Freud's notions of displacement and condensation to analyze the dream. If you are interested in dreams, read Jung's *Man and His Symbols* and use his concepts to analyze the same dream.

5. Take some image (graphic work) that interests you and analyze it in terms of the art/artist/audience/society/medium schema. How does this schema help you understand images and their impact better?

6. Collect a number of images that have different kinds of spatiality. What generalizations can you make about spatiality and taste?

7. Examine the lighting in various images. How do you think the lighting affects viewers? When you watch television programs, focus your attention on the lighting. What generalizations can you make about the kinds of lighting used in different kinds of shows?

8. What is your favorite color? Why?

9. Look at several packages in terms of the colors they use. What kind of feelings do these colors generate in you? Why do you think the artists who designed these packages chose those particular colors?

10. Take a package for some product and redesign it. In particular, change the colors. Explain what changes you made and why you made them. Remember, the function of packaging is to attract attention and convince people to purchase a given product.

11. Do some research on the psychological impact of perspective and write a short paper on it. Why did it take so long for people to "discover" perspective? What kind of feelings do you get when you look at an early work of art that doesn't use modern perspective?

12. What do you think is the relation that exists between the medium and the message? What effect does the medium have on the message? Are there cases in which a message is not affected, in significant ways, by the medium that carries it? If so, give some examples and explain your reasons for holding this view.

Photography:
The Captured Moment

Chapter 3

The Photograph

Photography was invented in 1839 by Daguerre and Niepce in France and, independently, by Henry Fox Talbot in England. The Daguerre method used sensitized metal (and could not be reproduced) while the Talbot method used a paper negative process that led, eventually, to modern photography as we now know it. The American George Eastman, who founded Eastman Kodak, made further developments that led to roll film, which was introduced in 1881 and led, ultimately, to the modern motion picture.

Photography involves the following processes:

1. Using a camera to take a picture on light-sensitive film
2. Developing or processing this film and making a negative
3. Using this negative to make prints on light-sensitive paper

The result of this process is the photograph, the dominant form of permanent image in the modern world.

A photograph can be defined as an image, in the form of a positive print, taken by a camera (a device with a lens and shutter) and reproduced, permanently, on a photosensitive surface. Cameras range from the cheap throwaway models currently being produced to very expensive German and Japanese models with powerful lenses and many automatic features.

Human visual perception is a far more complex and selective process than that by which a film records. Nevertheless the camera lens and the eye both register images — because of their sensitivity to light — at great speed and in the face of an immediate event. What the camera does and what the eye can never do, is to fix the appearance of that event. It removes its appearance from the flow of appearances and it preserves it . . . The camera saves a set of appearances from the otherwise inevitable supercession of further appearances. It holds them unchanging. And before the invention of the camera nothing could do this, except, in the mind's eye, the faculty of memory.

JOHN BERGER, *About Looking*

Genres in Photography

The term *genre* refers to a kind or type of art work that is found in some medium. We make a distinction between a medium, such as radio, television, or photography and the genres found in the medium. For example, television is a medium that comprises genres such as soap operas, commercials, news shows, sports programs, talk shows, etc. In the same light, photography is a medium that includes several different genres.

Art Photos

Works of fine art by great photographers who exploit the aesthetic elements in photography (to create works that are considered "high" art) are now found in the photography collections of many museums (Figure 3.1). The great photographers have generally worked in black and white — in many cases because color photography had not been developed when many of them were doing their work. Even now, there is a tendency for art photographers to work in black and white.

Snapshots

Photographs taken by ordinary people, typically showing their children growing up, sights seen in their travels, and special events are a form of personal documentation (Figure 3.2). Portraits can be art photos, but most often they are more formal versions of the snapshot.

Photojournalism

In newspapers and magazines photographs are used for their documentary and illustrative powers. These photographs show us the important events and people we read about and augment the material we get from the printed word.

Photodocumentaries

The photodocumentary is a visual form of sociology and anthropology meant to capture images of importance that social scientists and others can use to get a sense of what a group of people is like (Figure 3.3). We now consider it important to have a record of how people live: their homes, their clothes, the objects they have in their homes, the foods they eat, the rituals they participate in, etc. Scholarly journals published by visual anthropologists and visual sociologists are devoted to furthering the development of these disciplines. The camera is now an extremely

FIGURE 3.1
Formal portrait of President Ronald Reagan, by Pete Souza.

FIGURE 3.2
"Snapshot" of President Ronald Reagan. This photograph conveys an impression of Ronald Reagan different from that of the formal portrait in Figure 3.1. He is portrayed in a natural setting, has powerful arms, is informally dressed, and has a larger-than-life quality about him. Technically speaking, this photograph isn't really a snapshot but rather an informal shot that gives the feeling of being a snapshot and may be seen as an example of Reagan's ability to give people "illusions" about himself.

FIGURE 3.3
Anthropologists use photographs to record important information about the peoples and cultures they study. There is a specialty called visual anthropology, and there are journals devoted to this subject.

important element of field work for anthropologists and has revolutionized the way anthropologists work. (The same could be said for the Super 8 film camera and now the video camera.)

Commercial Photography

The use of photographs in advertisements, packaging, record covers, posters, and billboards is probably the dominant use of photography in contemporary society. The average American is exposed to huge numbers of these photographs each day.

As the result of the power of the photograph to record reality, oil painting has changed and artists no longer focus so directly on reality. It can be argued that the photograph indirectly led to such movements as Abstract Expressionism and Op Art, genres concerned not with being realistic and imitating reality, but rather with expressing emotions and feelings through the use of color, design, and related techniques.

The Problem of Objectivity

Because there are so many variables in photography—in terms of camera angles, use of light and dark, texture, and focus—we must recognize that a picture is always an *interpretation* of reality, not reality itself. A dozen photographers taking pictures of the same scene would come up with a dozen different views of it. The photographs would be similar as far as the subject matter is concerned but different as far as the actual photographs are concerned. Photography, though it is a mechanical process, does not automatically reproduce reality.

Consider the options photographers have at their disposal when they make photographs:

1. Lighting (flat, chiaroscuro, and gradations in between)
2. Focus (sharp, soft)
3. Composition (use of white space and other design factors)
4. Angle of the shot
5. Color (if color is used)

These options suggest that interpretative factors play a very large role in the creation of a photograph or series of photographs. Think, for example, of the difference between a mug shot taken in a prison and a portrait taken by a fine photographer (Figures 3.4 and 3.5).

Evidence and Glamorization

In a mug shot, photography is used to record a person's likeness in as simple and uncomplicated a manner as possible. In the portrait, photography is used to capture the essence of someone's personality and character—one might sometimes say to "glamorize" the person. These two poles—evidence and glamorization—are the extremes between which photography operates.

In Figure 3.6 a beautiful young woman (who happens to be a ballerina) is shown smiling and, from her pose, looking right at

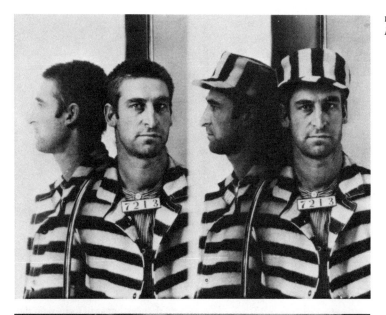

FIGURE 3.4
Mugshot No. 7213.

FIGURE 3.5
Portrait of a man on a chair. Notice the expression on his face, the stiffness of his pose, and the style of his clothing. All of these are signs that give us insights into the man and his personality.

us. She is tousling her hair, a nonverbal form of communication that has erotic implications. Her face is expressive and radiant, and the pupils of her eyes are slightly dilated (or enlarged), a sign generally held to be an unconscious indicator of sexual interest and excitement.

Desire can also be evoked by making allusion to certain scenes or stories or individuals that are part of our collective frame of reference and signify romance, love, and related matters: Cleopatra, Romeo and Juliet, Helen of Troy, Marilyn Monroe — the list is endless. As Tony Schwartz (1974:24–25) writes in *The Responsive Chord:*

> The critical task is to design our package of stimuli so that it resonates with information already stored with the individual and thereby induces the desired learning or behavioral effect. Resonance takes place when the stimuli put into our communication evoke meaning in a listener or viewer. That which we put into the communication has no meaning in itself. The meaning of our communication is what a listener or viewer gets out of his experience with the communicator's stimulus.

In other words, the photographs we see every day are stimuli that "activate" us by setting off the appropriate responsive chord. These photographs (and advertising in general) exploit what is already in our heads, the cultural lore we have stored up as a result of our education and experiences.

Connected with this desire is a latent dissatisfaction with ourselves the way we are as well as our hopes for a better self in the future (when we have purchased whatever product or service is being advertised). And so we live our lives, suspended in a sense, between the mug shot of everyday reality and the portrait and the life of glamor and romance that it promises us.

The Pose: Figure and Ground

Some photographs are taken randomly, as a shot suggests itself in the course of a given day or experience. But others — in particular, the portrait — are posed. We all like to think that we can "read" personality or character just by looking at a person's face, as if that face recorded or stored up, in some magical way, that person's experiences. Although we may often be able to do this to a degree, in many cases poses are a representation not of character but rather of personality. The term *personality* comes from the word *persona,* which means mask. Our personalities are masks that we present to the world, and the photograph may be capturing this mask and not our "real" selves.

FIGURE 3.6
Portrait of Alaina Albertson. Notice the expressiveness of this woman's smile, her pose, and the way her gaze focuses on the viewer.

How do we read a photograph for personality or character? (Or is the question "How do we misread a photograph?") For one thing, a person in a portrait is often shown with a background that helps define that person. Lawyers are frequently portrayed in their libraries, with rows and rows of law books behind them, suggesting the knowledge (and with knowledge, power) that this person has. We find portraits of poor people in their shacks, with only the barest of furniture or possessions; this ground helps define the figures. So the ground helps define the figure, just as the figure helps define the ground. This background and the objects in it provide us with information that helps us gain an understanding of the person being portrayed.

Second, there is the matter of the way the person looks. We all have notions about what having blonde hair or a weak chin or being gap-toothed or very thin or fat or short or tall signifies. "Conventional wisdom" tells us what facial features and body shapes mean, and we apply this "wisdom" (which, of course, is often wrong) to the people we see in portraits (Figures 3.7 and 3.8). Facial expression is another way of conveying information — through such things as a smile, a frown, a look of puzzlement, or stoic resignation. We all can empathize with others since we reveal different emotions via our facial expressions.

Third, body language helps us read photographs. We are now aware that there is a whole world of nonverbal communication that exists and that we are always communicating, whether we say a word or not. Thus body language generates messages that we all can interpret. In addition to facial expression and body language, there are various props (in the theatrical sense of term) people use to generate impressions. Some of the most important are:

1. *Hairstyle.* Crewcuts, punk, long hair, the "Ollie North" look, etc., all convey information about a person. With women, long, straight hair conveys a different impression than does short curly hair. And as time progresses and hairstyles become popular or fade, we read a person via hairstyles, which suggest a person is "with it" or "square."
2. *Eyeglasses.* The style of eyeglasses tells us about the taste or life-style of the person wearing them. Now that contact lenses are so popular, a person who chooses to wear eyeglasses might be trying to create a certain impression.
3. *Fashion.* We have learned in recent years that fashion provides information and that there are various ways one dresses for "power." Think of the difference between a dark, pin-striped three-piece suit and jeans and a tee shirt.

FIGURE 3.7
Portrait of Roy Cohn. Cohn was a celebrated and, some would say, "notorious" figure in American politics. What impressions do you get when you examine his face? What leads you to have these feelings?

FIGURE 3.8
Portrait of Truman Capote. Capote was an important literary figure and a fascinating personality. Examine his face the same way you examined Cohn's, and see what impressions you get. Do we "read" faces on the basis of what we know about the people who have been photographed or do we "read" facial expressions, poses, and other signs as a means of coming to conclusions about them?

The Problem of Objectivity | **67**

4. *Jewelry.* The kind of jewelry one wears is a means of impression management. What does it mean when men wear earrings? What if a woman wears many pairs of earrings? Think about class rings and wedding rings. Jewelry or its lack is an important prop.
5. *Makeup.* A woman with a great deal of makeup seems to be quite different from a woman with no makeup at all (the "natural" look). Long polished nails convey a certain image —associated with glamour—in our minds.
6. *Briefcases, attache cases, bags,* etc. These objects also generate impressions and are used by people for the purpose of impression management.

When we look at a photograph of a person or a group of persons there is a great deal to decipher if we are to get the full meaning of the photograph (Figure 3.9). We use our faces, our

FIGURE 3.9
Linda Rich, *Stella Foods.* This photograph of a food store owned by the Kostis family for twenty-one years offers an incredible amount of visual detail. Contrast this store with the sterility of the modern supermarket, for example.

bodies, our clothes, and objects to create certain impressions in other people. To read photographs correctly requires background information or what might be called "consumer cultural literacy." If you do not recognize, for example, that a briefcase has the logo of an expensive Italian fashion house, you've missed something its owner wanted to convey.

Technical Aspects of the Photograph

Focus

Focus refers to the clarity of an image or part of an image. We use the term *depth of field* to refer to objects in focus in an image. This depth of field varies, depending upon the kind of lens we use in the camera. We get greater depth of field with wide-angle lenses than with narrow-angle lenses, as Figures 3.10 and 3.11 demonstrate. We can use focus to emphasize certain things and deemphasize other things or to generate certain impressions. Thus, a soft focus is associated with the romantic and related emotional states and is often used in cosmetic advertisements, which sell magic and fantasy. On the other hand, very sharp and clear focus is connected with science and pure rationality.

FIGURE 3.10
Hard focus. Photo of Jan, unmodified.

FIGURE 3.11
Soft focus. Photo of Jan, modified by computer to achieve softened effect.

FIGURE 3.10

FIGURE 3.11

Grain

The term *grain* refers to the prominence of the minute dots that make up a photograph. Grainy photographs are associated with snapshots and photographs taken by chance or in difficult situations. Thus we associate grain with realism and honesty. We do not use grainy photographs as a rule; and so when they are used, it suggests that something unusual has transpired or is being communicated.

Shot Angle

Angle refers to where the camera is relative to the subject of the photograph. A shot that "looks up" to the subject conveys a different impression (such as reverence?) than one that "looks down" on (and is superior to?) the subject (Figure 3.12). When we photograph people, the shot angle is quite important. A full-face shot conveys a different impression than does a three-quarter face shot or a profile (Figure 3.13).

With the full-face shot, we find that the person being photographed is, in a sense, looking us directly in the eyes; and thus this pose suggests honesty and candor. The three-quarter face shot has been interpreted by Roland Barthes to suggest a person of vision, who is looking beyond us to the future. The person in

FIGURE 3.12
Angle of shot. A three-quarter view taken from above.

FIGURE 3.13
In these "stylized" portraits there are a
variety of effects generated by the use of
the techniques available to the
photographer. Photographs are not simple
reproductions of reality but are stylized
representations of reality.

the profile shot becomes an object of scrutiny, someone who is looked at. We find this angle in mug shots and in certain portraits, where a person's profile strikes the photographer as the best way of portraying the subject.

Kinds of Shots

Here we are concerned with the length or distance of the camera from the subject. Let me list some of the most important shots, assuming that we are photographing a person, though we could be photographing an object or a building or a general landscape:

1. *The extreme close-up.* This might portray only part of a person's face.
2. *The close-up.* This generally would include the face but not much else of a person.
3. *The medium shot.* Here we have the face and part of the torso.
4. *The long shot.* Here we have the entire body and some of the surroundings.
5. *The extreme long shot.* Here the figures are relatively small and much of the surroundings is shown. This shot functions as an establishing shot and suggests the context in which a given person or group of persons is to be found.

Each of these shots has a particular function and conveys a certain kind of message. The extreme close-up is very personal and intimate and is meant to give us insights into the personality of the person being photographed. As we move away from the camera in a perpendicular line (known as the Z-axis) we become less involved with personality and more with background or context. Close-up, medium, and long shots of a building are shown in Figures 3.14, 3.15, and 3.16.

Color

Photographers can use different kinds of coated lenses to manipulate color. They can deepen or emphasize certain colors and minimize others. Thus color is one more variable that photographers can play with to create the effects they wish — such as making food photographs look so mouth-wateringly good.

Composition

When photographers print their negatives, they have an additional opportunity to manipulate images. They can create a composition that pleases them, by selecting only a certain portion of

FIGURE 3.14
Close-up of the White House (above). Here we see just a portion of the White House.

FIGURE 3.15
Medium shot of the White House (top right). In this shot we see the entire White House, but nothing else.

FIGURE 3.16
Long shot of the White House (right). Here we see the fountains in front of the White House and a bit of the environs. We are considerably farther away from the White House than we were in the medium shot.

the negative to use, a process known as *cropping*. A given negative can yield any number of different photographs, depending upon the aesthetic interests of the photographer (Figure 3.17).

By playing with focus and depth of field, shot angles, kinds of shots, grain, color, and composition, photographers are able to create many different effects and generate many different meanings in a given situation (Figures 3.18 and 3.19). Photography is not a reflection or an imitation of reality but an interpretation of reality. Therefore, seeing isn't always believing, since photographs only reveal, ultimately, what photographers want their photographs to reveal.

In recent years, as a result of developments in computer imaging, photographs can now be manipulated in remarkable ways, and changes made to them cannot be detected by the human

FIGURE 3.17
Photograph cropped three ways. Cropping involves selecting that part of an image to be used and plays an important part in the design process. By cropping, photographers can emphasize certain things and shape the composition of the shot to their liking. A given negative, then, can yield a number of different photographs. The kinds of screens used to reproduce photographs also generate different effects, as the examples reproduced show.

(A)

(B)

eye. As a result, photographs no longer can be thought of as evidence, since with computers almost anything is possible. Again, seeing is not believing and what you get is not always what someone saw.

As has been suggested earlier, what we see is, to a great degree, affected by what we know—the degree of cultural literacy we have, the extent to which we can understand allusions and references to things, can evaluate the socioeconomic significance of props and objects and are in tune with the same codes as the photographer (or, in the case of advertisements, the copywriter and art director responsible for a given advertisement).

Advertising Photography and Oil Painting

In *Ways of Seeing,* the English art critic John Berger points out that many of the devices found in advertising photography come from oil painting. He writes (1972:138):

> Compare the images of publicity [the English term for advertising] and paintings in this book, or take a picture magazine, or walk down a smart shopping street looking at the window displays, and then turn over the pages of an illustrated museum catalogue, and notice how similarly messages are conveyed by the two media. A systematic study needs to be made of this. Here we can do no more than indicate a few areas where the similarity of the devices and aims is particularly striking.

A partial list of the items mentioned by Berger follows. Notice the degree to which information *in the mind of the observer* is crucial to interpreting these images correctly:

The gestures of models (mannequins) and mythological figures.
The romantic use of nature (leaves, trees, water) to create a place where innocence can be refound.
The exotic and nostalgic attraction of the Mediterranean.
The poses taken up to denote stereotypes of women: serene mother (madonna), free-wheeling secretary (actress, king's mistress), perfect hostess (spectator-owner's wife), sex-object (Venus, nymph surprised), etc. The special sexual emphasis given to women's legs.
The materials particularly used to indicate luxury: engraved metal, furs, polished leather, etc.
The gestures and embraces of lovers, arranged frontally for the benefit of the spectator.
The physical stance of men conveying wealth and virility.

All of these images come from the world of oil painting, which had the mission (before the development of photography) of celebrating private property and suggesting, as Berger puts it, that "you are what you have" (Figure 3.20). This task has now been taken over by photography and, through the institution of advertising (a hundred-billion-dollar industry in America), is spread to the masses.

What advertising does, Berger suggests, is make us marginally dissatisfied with our lot so that we pin our hopes on a better future by purchasing products and services that will enhance our sense of well-being. For the working classes, advertising promises (1972:145) "a personal transformation through the function of the product it is selling (Cinderella); middle-class publicity promises a transformation of relationships through a general atmosphere created by an ensemble of products (The Enchanted Palace)." These implied promises are tied to the power of the image to create desire as well as to generate a certain amount of anxiety, and the two are linked together. Wherever we find desire, we also find anxiety.

The Image and Capitalism

We can push this analysis of the image and society up one level on the ladder of abstraction now by examining the ideas of Susan Sontag. She suggests in her book *On Photography* that capitalist societies need photographic images. She writes (1973:178,179):

> A capitalist society requires a culture based on images. It needs to furnish vast amounts of entertainment in order to stimulate buying and anesthetize the injuries of class, race, and sex. And it needs to gather unlimited amounts of information, the better to exploit natural resources, increase productivity, keep order, make war, give jobs to bureaucrats. The camera's twin capacities, to subjectivize reality and to objectify it, ideally serve these needs and strengthen them. Cameras define reality in the two ways essential to the workings of an advanced industrial society: as a spectacle (for masses) and as an object of surveillance (for rulers). The production of images also furnishes a ruling ideology. Social change is replaced by a change in images. The freedom to consume a plurality of images and goods is equated with freedom itself. The narrowing of free political choice to free economic consumption requires the unlimited production and consumption of images.

From Sontag's perspective, the photographic image takes on rather ominous and sinister proportions. Whether her analysis is correct is a matter for debate; but she does point out how powerful and useful the photographic image is and the complicated role these images play in modern societies.

FIGURE 3.20
William Beckman, *Diana IV*, 1981. Which stereotype of women, as discussed by John Berger, applies to this painting?

The Photograph and Narcissism

The photograph is used as a record of our existence and the existence of our loved ones. Thus, when we have young children, we take many pictures of them as they develop. We also take pictures of ourselves on trips as proof, so to speak, that we actually made the trip and as a way of indirectly indicating that we exist and are participating in history. This explains why we often take snapshots of our loved ones (or induce others to take pictures of us and our loved ones) in front of hotels, statues, palaces, churches, temples, and other sites of significance.

There is also an autoerotic element to the photographs we take of ourselves. If modern societies subject us to the stresses John Berger and Susan Sontag write about, there is some measure of consolation in retreating into ourselves, into what might be described as an imagistic form of narcissism. Like Narcissus, the mythological figure who fell in love with his own reflection, our photographs do have a powerful self-referential eroticism about them. We may not go as far as Narcissus, but we do have strong feelings about our image, as presented to us by photographs.

That might explain why we complain, so often, about photographs taken of us that they "don't look like" us, aren't flattering, or don't do justice to us. One reason for this stems from the difference between the idealized image of ourselves that we "see" in the mirror and the harsh reality of the photograph. It is, of course, possible to have a photograph that really doesn't look like oneself; this happens from time to time.

And some photographs are terribly unflattering, due to the lighting or camera angle and that kind of thing. But more often than not, it is not the photograph that lies, but we who lie to ourselves. Or we lie to others by using photographs of ourselves taken many years back. It is quite natural to wish to present ourselves to others in the best possible light, which — in the case of a portrait — often means (ironically) the least possible light.

Conclusions

The photograph is, then, an extremely enigmatic and complicated item. It has enormous power, which means that we must always consider the ethics involved in taking photographs and using them. We use the photographic image in numerous ways and photographic images pervade our modern society — making it what it is and, some would say, giving us images of ourselves that shape our sense of identity and our sociopolitical order.

Certain people (often in what we describe as nonliterate cultures) believe that if you have an image of a person, you have some kind of occult power over that person. We laugh at this and label it as ignorant or magical thinking, but if we consider the power of the photographic image more closely, these notions may not be so wrong. In the beginning was the word; shortly after that came the image, and when we put the two together, all kinds of remarkable things started to happen.

Applications

1. Do you consider photography to be a fine art? If so, why? If not, why not?

2. What do you think is the difference between a snapshot and a photograph?

3. If you have access to photographs taken of you when you were growing up, examine them and try to determine what they tell you about yourself and your family.

4. People frequently claim that photographs taken of them don't really look like them. Do you think this is correct? If so, how do you explain it? If not, why not?

5. Why is it that photographs have the power to evoke strong emotional responses in people? How would you explain this?

6. It has been suggested that photographs are very useful documents for people who want to find out about a culture. How can we use photographs this way? What do we look for? Find some photographs that you think have cultural significance and analyze them. What do you find?

7. Do you think a photograph can capture the essence of a person or merely the image of a person? Explain your position and justify your answer.

8. To what degree does what we know and bring to a photograph affect the way we respond to and interpret a photograph? If you never heard of the Holocaust and were shown pictures of people in the concentration camps, would the pictures have the same impact? Explain your answer.

9. Pretend you are a tourist and take a series of photographs that a tourist would take in your hometown or some area near you. Now pretend you are a visual anthropologist and take another series of photographs that an anthropologist

would take in the same place. What differences do you find in the two series of photographs?

10. Assume you are commissioned by a photography magazine to take some portraits of your friends. Take some portraits in which you pose your subjects and try to capture their personality and character. After you have taken the photographs answer these questions: What problems did you confront in taking these photographs? How well were you able to capture the personality and character of your subjects?

11. Use your camera to document a typical day in your life. What does this exercise reveal about you and your everyday life? Assuming your classmates do this exercise, what do their photographs reveal about their lives? Did you discover anything about your life or the lives of your friends that was surprising? How did you make sure you weren't giving a false impression of your everyday life? How did you decide what photographs to take and what matters to leave out?

12. Choose some subject that interests you and that has interesting pictorial possibilities and do a photo-essay on it. What is it like to write about a topic that you have also photographed? Was your photo-essay shaped primarily by what you wanted to show or what you wanted to say? Explain your answer.

Film: The Moving Image   Chapter 4

Motion Pictures

Movies have had a curious history. In their earliest days they were looked upon as miraculous but rather primitive amusements. Later on they were seen as entertainments, but not as a serious or significant art form. Now, the motion picture is considered an extremely important art form. Many films are seen by scholars as great works of art, and many directors are treated as great creative artists (or, as the French put it, "auteurs"). So the motion picture has come a long way and has moved from being a popular art form to an elite art form. In recent years, with the development of semiotics, the motion picture has been studied not only in terms of what it reflects about society and the ideological messages it carries but also, and perhaps primarily, in terms of how meaning is generated by what might be described as the grammar of film—the various kinds of shots and editing techniques that directors use to give shape to their vision.

A motion picture is defined in *Webster's Ninth New Collegiate Dictionary* as follows:

> a series of pictures projected on a screen in rapid succession with objects shown in successive positions slightly changed so as to produce the optical effect of a continuous picture in which the objects move . . . . .*

* By permission. From *Webster's Ninth New Collegiate Dictionary* © 1987 by Merriam-Webster Inc., publisher of the Merriam-Webster ® dictionaries.

Like painting and sculpture, film employs line, texture, color, form, volume, and mass, as well as subtle interplays of light and shadow. Many of the rules of photographic composition followed in the motion picture are similar to those applied in painting and sculpture. Like the drama, film communicates visually through dramatic action, gesture, and expression, and verbally through dialogue. Like music and poetry, film utilizes subtle and complex rhythms, and like poetry, in particular, it communicates through images, metaphors and symbols. Like pantomime, film concentrates upon the moving image, and like the dance, that moving image has certain rhythmic qualities.

JOSEPH M. BOGGS, *The Art of Watching Films*

What we see is a succession of discrete frames, projected at a rate of twenty-four frames per second (normal speed) that offers the illusion of motion—because an afterimage lingers in the eye that connects all the images together.

There are several variations on the speed at which scenes are filmed. Scenes filmed at greater-than-normal speed (but projected at twenty-four frames a second) seem to move slowly; this is called slow motion. When the reverse happens, and scenes are filmed at slower-than-normal speed and projected at twenty-four frames a second, we have fast motion (sometimes called "speeded" motion). There is also a device known as the "freeze-frame," where one image is continued for a period of time, stopping motion. This powerful effect is often used as a transitional device.

The basic unit of film is the frame, which is a discrete image. (Unlike film, television does not have frames.) The existence of discrete frames makes it possible for film scholars to examine films in considerable detail and to reproduce certain frames of significance (Figure 4.1). Frames contain an enormous amount of material—they are really analogous to the photographic images discussed in Chapter 3. But the complete motion picture involves combinations of frames and is based on what might be called shots (to be discussed shortly).

Films are not shot in sequence; different scenes are shot in different order, but all are merged into the proper sequence at the end of shooting—a process known as editing (Figure 4.2). Editing involves deciding how to arrange the segments of the film as a means of shaping the emotional responses of the viewers. A given amount of film footage, from the original shoots, can be shaped in many different ways, depending upon the taste and aesthetic sensibilities of the film editor.

In a certain sense, a film can be looked upon as a work designed to generate certain desired emotional responses in people. This view is somewhat of an oversimplification, but it points out the fact that film makers are after various effects; in fact, they often start with a given desired effect and work backwards, trying to figure out how to achieve the effect.

FIGURE 4.1
F. W. Murnau, detail of still from *Nosferatu*, 1922. Notice how this shot conveys horror. We look up at the vampire figure; he has sunken eyes, a deathlike expression on his face, and long, hideously curved fingernails.

Conventions of Film Editing

There are certain conventions or codes of editing that we all learn by experience, from watching numerous motion pictures. These conventions include:

FIGURE 4.2
Sergei Eisenstein, *The Battleship Potemkin,* 1925. These stills, taken from the great Russian film, show how directors edit films — they vary the shots to provide information and to shape the emotional responses of viewers.

1. *The wipe.* A new image replaces a previous one by a defined horizontal, vertical or diagonal line that "wipes" the old image off the screen. This creates a sharp break with past action.
2. *The dissolve.* One image gradually fades or "dissolves" into a new image. This less radical break with past action is often used to suggest the passage of a good deal of time.
3. *The fade-out or fade-in.* The image gradually fades away to black (an empty screen) or fades in from an empty screen. Often fade-outs and fade-ins are combined but this need not be done.
4. *The flip-frame.* Here the frame appears to flip over into a new scene.
5. *The cut.* Here a sequence is stopped, and a complete new image is shown. When a number of cuts are used, to suggest a number of things going on at the same time (simultaneity) and excitement, it is called quick cutting.
6. *The defocus shot.* Here a scene ends by moving out of focus and a new scene begins out of focus and moves into clear focus. This device links the two scenes in the viewer's mind.

All of these devices are analogous to punctuation in writing; they are the means by which the director indicates (though not overtly) to the viewers how they should relate scenes to one another. If you do not know these editing conventions and what each signifies, you are likely to misinterpret the film. As we grow up and watch films, we all learn, through trial and error, what the conventions are and how to respond to them.

Shots and Shot Relationships

We have already discussed shots in the chapter on photography. Because of the nature of film, however, there are some additional topics to be dealt with here.

The Zoom Shot

Film makes possible the zoom shot, in which we use a lens to move in, smoothly, closer and closer on a subject, from a long shot or medium shot, until we arrive at a close-up (Figure 4.3). The zoom shot has the effect of intensifying an image, of making it possible to inspect an object or a person's face more closely. It is a message from the director that we must pay special attention to something and look for something that will be revealed to us.

FIGURE 4.3
Representation of a zoom shot sequence, in which we move from a long shot to a medium shot to a close-up.

There is a suggestion of intimacy. Inexperienced directors sometimes become "zoom crazy" and use the zoom so often that it loses its novelty and impact and viewers become discomforted.

In the same way, a reverse zoom, in which the camera moves away from a close-up of an object or a person, conveys the opposite emotion. Here we are being asked to take a larger view and to look at the big picture. Thus, this shot is meant to give us a picture of relationships and the overall structure of a situation. It suggests reason and distancing, not emotional involvement.

The Reaction Shot

Here the camera focuses on the reaction of a character to something said (the dialogue) or an event in the film. The reaction shot reveals, visually, how an important figure in the story has responded to something. This shot is meant to shape our perception of things and our emotional responses to the dialogue or events that have just transpired.

Montage

This concept was developed by the film theorist and director Sergei Eisenstein, who used it in a number of different ways. In essence, Eisenstein argues in *Film Form* (1949:49), "montage is an idea that arises from the collision of independent shots—

shots even opposite to one another . . . " Thus we derive meaning in film from seeing shots in combination. One shot is, for all practical purposes, a photograph; but when shots are *combined* in certain sequences, we are led to have certain ideas or emotional responses. This explains, in part, the power of MTV, which often is exciting and experimental in its use of shots and editing.

Montage can involve such visual matters as graphic elements, planes, volumes, spatiality, images of motion, etc. By playing off one shot (or aspects of that shot) against another, we produce the meaning or effect that Eisenstein considers to be the basis of montage and ultimately of film (Figure 4.4). This calls to mind the notion of the Swiss linguist Saussure, who argued in his *Course in General Linguistics* (1966:117) that "concepts are purely differential and defined not by their positive content but negatively by their relations with the other terms of the system." An image by itself can be made to mean anything and it is only when we see this image or shot placed in relationship to another image or shot that we get a specific emotion or idea.

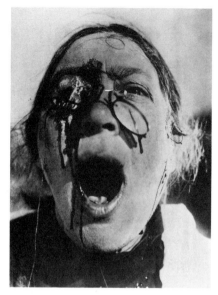

FIGURE 4.4
Sergei Eisenstein, still from *The Battleship Potemkin,* 1925. This image is one of his most famous. It shows a woman after she has been shot, with her blood spurting out. This and other images from this great film conveyed Eisenstein's sense of the horror of life under the czar.

Color

Originally films were black-and-white. When color film was introduced it was something of a novelty; and seeing a color film was a special occasion. Films would advertise, for example, that they were in technicolor; and color films, because they were unusual, had a distinctive appeal and quality. Now, with few exceptions, all films are made in color. This means that black-and-white films now are unusual and signify that a film is old, a documentary, or an "art" film.

From our discussion in Chapter 2, we realize that color can generate powerful emotional responses, especially when combined with other elements of film. So color (or, in some cases, the lack of color) is one more tool used to enhance and intensify our responses to images.

Because of the arbitrary relationship that exists between a signifier (such as the use of color) and what is signified (for example, madness) we should not automatically assume, for example, that black-and-white is a preferred medium for showing the "darker" elements of the psyche than color. It has been pointed out, for example, that the extremely rich coloration of the film *Blue Velvet* signified emotional disorientation and pathology equally as well as did the use of shadows and distorted images in black-and-white films from earlier times.

Sound

The first films did not have sound and relied on the images and captions or printed words to carry the narrative. The coming of sound, with *The Jazz Singer* in 1927, changed film dramatically, for now it was possible to use dialogue, sound effects, and music to shape the viewers' responses to a film.

Spoken Dialogue

The conversation that characters carry on in a film is dialogue. Dialogue is tied to scenes, generally speaking, not to frames (which are single images). When the scene — which is a segment of a story with certain characters in a particular place — changes, so does the dialogue.

The dialogue tells us what people are doing and often, by inference, what they are thinking. Thus dialogue helps the visual images we see carry the story along. Without sound, we can still get a pretty good idea of what is happening in a film, but our understanding is crude and simplistic. Often there is a pattern of shots and countershots or reaction shots (or reverse-angle shots) that matches the pattern of conversation we see in a scene. Using these conventions directors are able to let us know what the different characters are thinking (or seem to be thinking) and how they are responding to the conversation. It should be noted that film dialogue, like most conversation, is characterized by sentence fragments, interruptions, and overlapping speech. We do not, as a rule, always wait for others to stop speaking or speak in complete and beautifully structured sentences. And the dialogue generally is used to add something to the visual image, not to repeat the information the visual image offers us; the dialogue should add to the narrative but not replace the image.

We must also recognize that the language used in dialogue and the quality of a character's voice also tell us a great deal. The human voice has an intrinsic capacity to generate emotions that adds, then, to the power of the image — which explains why the motion picture is such a powerful medium.

Narration

In some films, such as documentaries, we find narration, in which a speaker (or several speakers) off the screen provides us with information relevant to the images we are seeing. Often we have both narration and dialogue, as a narrator sets a scene for us and then the characters involved act out the scene. Sometimes the narrator is also part of the action and steps in and out of the film to offer his or her comments. The narrator, as someone who is distanced from the action (even if only momentarily), can tell us things, offer opinions, and act as a kind of omniscient presence.

Narrators fill in gaps in a story's narrative line, provide important background information, tell us what we should think about various characters (and often what various characters are thinking), frame stories, and provide a tone to a story. As such they are very useful in all kinds of films — whether they be dramatic films or documentaries or mixtures such as docudramas. The presence of a narrator suggests that a story or film is realistic and suggests that it has documentary elements in it.

Sound Effects

These devices, which imitate the sounds associated with given phenomena, make a film seem realistic and natural. They also function as cues that shape our emotional responses. Thus, for example, a film about space might have a scene of a rocket blasting off and the awesome power of this series of sounds strikes us. In the same vein, if the sound we get does not correspond to our expectations and does not "go" with the event, we are immediately aroused and made suspicious.

There is some question about whether specific sounds always have a predictable effect upon people. Semiotics would suggest that this is *not* the case: a given sound — such as a shriek — can be used, depending upon the situation, to suggest joy and happiness or dread and terror. Recall that Saussure explained that a sign (which he defined as a sound or object) was arbitrarily or conventionally related to a given signifier or meaning. So any sound can be made to mean anything.

In *How to Read a Film,* James Monaco (1977:180,181) cites a French film theorist, Christian Metz, on the "five channels of information in a film: (1) the visual image; (2) print and other graphics; (3) speech; (4) music; (5) noise (sound effects). Interestingly, the majority of these channels are auditory rather than visual." And, he continues, there are only two continuous channels in this list — the visual image and noise/sound effects.

Sound in film is all-pervasive and helps create locales (room sound) and a sense of time. And, as we have developed technology with stereo, Dolby systems, etc., the power of sound in film has been augmented.

Music

The music found in the background of films plays a very important role, and many producers argue that often the music in a film makes the difference between a hit and a failure. Music is used to key the responses of viewers to particular scenes. This is done through the use of motifs — passages that become linked to certain kinds of events.

What happens, generally speaking, is that we are taught to associate certain musical motifs with certain events or kinds of events, and then these motifs can be used to trigger certain responses in us — we are, so to speak, conditioned and respond accordingly (the same way Pavlov's dogs were taught to associate a bell with being fed and thus were conditioned to salivate when they heard the bell). Music has the power to speak directly to our emotions, so it helps intensify and dramatize scenes and augments the visual images that we see.

As in the case of sound effects, in almost all cases it is the association that is crucial, not some intrinsic quality in the music itself that automatically generates a specific emotional response in everyone who hears it.

Special Visual Effects

A number of things can be done to affect the visual image, from simulated events (what we commonly describe as "special effects") to holding the camera by hand and getting a certain look. In some cases we keep the camera stationary and move the camera head or use a zoom lens; in other cases, we move the camera and its support in various ways (Figure 4.5).

The Hand-Held Camera

When a camera operator holds a camera and shoots with it, there is an unsteady, jerky quality to the resultant image that suggests this is the kind of film we might get from a spectator at a scene who happened to have a camera on hand. The lack of precision or absolute clarity engenders a sense of veracity and truthfulness. So directors use hand-held cameras when they want to counter the kind of image they get from using mounted cameras.

Camera Movement

A pan involves a camera head travelling horizontally across a person, object, or scene; a tilt involves a camera head travelling vertically across a person, object, or scene; a roll involves a camera flipping an image of a person, object, or scene about. A roll is much more disorienting than the other kinds of shots. A truck (left or right) involves the horizontal movement of the camera and its support in front of a given scene; a dolly in or dolly out involves the actual movement of the camera and its support either toward or away from a scene; and an arc is a movement, semicircular in nature, of a camera and its support around a given scene.

Each of these shots creates a different effect. For example, the pan is a kind of inspection of a terrain; the tilt is more focused and direct. And the roll is meant to disorient and surprise the viewer.

Deep Focus and Shallow Focus

Deep focus refers to a large depth of field, in which objects close to the camera as well as those at a considerable distance from it are

FIGURE 4.5
Detail from Gilbert Shelton's *The Fabulous Furry Freak Brothers,* "Getting Out the Vote." Film makers have learned a great deal about varying their shots from studying frames in comic strips.

in clear focus. This clarity imparts a very strong sense of realism to a scene. Orson Welles used deep focus to stunning effect in his masterpiece *Citizen Kane* (Figure 4.6). Shallow focus, which involves having only a small part of an image in focus, is a technique of directing the attention of the viewer to something in particular, by having it in focus and everything else out of focus (Figure 4.7).

FIGURE 4.6
Orson Welles, still from *Citizen Kane*, 1941. This is an example of deep focus in which the details at the end of the table are as clear as the ones at the front of the table. Note, also, how the ice sculptures frame the image and almost seem to be members of the party.

FIGURE 4.7
Shallow focus.

The Jump Cut

With this editing device the editor slices out the middle or some part of a sequence and cuts or "jumps" from one section of it to another. This process helps shape the rhythm of the scene and speed it up. We learn the convention of the jump cut in the comic book. The artists cannot provide all the intervening shots, so they jump from one scene to another and allow us to fill in the gaps in our own imaginations via the process of psychological closure.

The Power of the Film Image

When we see a film in a theatre, we find ourselves "captives" (in a sense) in a large room with others, where we sit in darkness watching huge images on a gigantic screen. The very scale of the images we watch in movie-houses itself has an impact; that is why you get a much different feeling when you see a film in a theatre than you do when you see that same film on a VCR in your home. And the quality of the audio system in the theatre is also much better, which intensifies the experience.

But there is something in movies, wherever you see them, that also strikes responsive chords in viewers; it is the fact that we are, generally speaking, watching stories featuring human beings, with whom we can empathize and to whom we often have (and this is often unconscious) a sensual or erotic response. As Martin Esslin suggests in *The Age of Television* (1982:30):

> . . . drama is basically erotic. Actors give the spectators who watch them a great deal of pleasure simply by being interesting, memorable, or beautiful specimens of humanity. Quite apart from their artistic or intellectual accomplishments, actors are people who exhibit their physical presence to the public . . . In a sense all actors are exhibitionists: they enjoy being seen, being found appealing and worth looking at. Conversely audiences of dramas are also, in a certain sense, voyeurs.

The power of this generally submerged and subliminal erotic relationship we have with actors and actresses is such that it is easy to identify with them and to internalize their values and beliefs.

There is an element of what is called *scopophilia* (loving by looking) at play here, which helps explain why facial expressions play so important a role in drama. We are all fascinated by others, and want to know as much as we can about them, their personalities, their hidden selves. Thus we scrutinize their facial expressions (and take note of everything else, I might add) as a means of getting to know characters (Figure 4.8). In discussing television, Esslin writes (1982:29), "The ability of TV to transmit personality is, undoubtedly, the secret of its immense power. For human beings are insatiable in their interest about other human beings." The same could be said about films.

It may also be that the sense of isolation and separation many people feel in modern societies exacerbates our hunger for relationships (even if only mass-mediated pseudo-relationships) and makes movies and television drama much more important aspects of our lives than they might otherwise be. Social scientists use the term "para-social relationships" for the feeling many people have that they really know actors and actresses.

The Nature of Drama

Films generally tell stories; that is, they are narratives in which we find characters pursuing their own interests and often in conflict with one another. Thus, the element of action is added to that of personality (and, often, demonstrates personality), enabling us to make "a willing suspension of disbelief" and enter into the drama, forgetting that we are spectators watching actors and actresses pretending to be certain characters doing various things. Usually in dramas there is a conflict (or many conflicts) between characters (who may be heroes and heroines and villains and villainesses) and a satisfactory resolution to the conflict.

The pacing of many films, the rapidity of the action sequences, and the nature of the dangers presented to the heroes and heroines excite us. Such excitement is inherent in films such as *Raiders of the Lost Ark* and others in that genre, in which one action scene leads to another one in rapid succession (Figure 4.9). These are very similar in structure to commercials full of quick cuts. The very rapidity of the cutting generates a sense of excitement.

In many respects film and television dramas are like dreams, in which all kinds of remarkable things occur (Figure 4.10). According to Freudian theory, our dreams occur in the form of discontinuous images that we "put together" when we recall them, via a process known as secondary elaboration.

A dream would be very much like a series of jump cuts or comic strip panels, and our minds fill in the gaps. What makes dreams (and films) powerful is that they are full of symbols that

FIGURE 4.8
Sylvester Stallone, *Rocky,* 1976. This close-up on the face of Stallone helps create a sense of involvement with the character and conveys a sense of what is motivating him.

FIGURE 4.9
Steven Spielberg, *Raiders of the Lost Ark,* 1981. This film featured an almost endless sequence of life-threatening situations that the hero, Harrison Ford, had to overcome.

FIGURE 4.10
Ingmar Bergman, *The Seventh Seal,* 1956.
Bergman's use of symbolism and the
striking photography give this film a
dreamlike quality and incredible dramatic
power.

speak to repressed or unconscious elements in our psyches and
that evoke powerful responses. Generally these symbols have a
sexual content that is hidden or masked by the processes of
displacement and condensation. If there are erotic aspects to
watching film and television, as Esslin suggests, there are even
more powerful sexual aspects to our dreams—the dramas that
we create in our own minds as we sleep. In our dreams, we are
not only the producers and directors but also the actors and
actresses.

Conclusions

Film is a very powerful medium and a very complex one. In
recent years, with the development of semiotics (often in alliance
with psychoanalytic theory and Marxist theory), we have become interested in how films generate meaning in people and
have discovered that it is a very complicated matter. At one time
we used to think that a given film had a given meaning and that it
was the function of the film critic to point out that meaning. Now
we know that everyone doesn't interpret a given film the same
way. What we see and get out of a film is related to what we
know and have experienced in life.

Thus, if a film is full of parodies of the work of other directors and includes allusions to historical events and we don't recognize the parodies or know what is alluded to, we will not get as much out of that film as will someone who does recognize the parodies and allusions. The more you know, the more you see and understand. That is why it is now fashionable to talk about audiences "reading" films and to suggest that audiences must play a significant role in making sense of a film. The film does not bear the entire burden; instead, it cooperates with us, so to speak.

This shows why an understanding of the principles of visual communication is so important. When we study a film (or that important genre of film or television we call the commercial), the more we know about lighting and camera angles and kinds of shots and color and symbolism, the better we will be able to understand how it works and what is good and bad about it.

Of course when we go to the movies, to enjoy ourselves, we just watch the film and hope to be entertained by it. But later on, if we discuss the film with friends or study it, we can employ the repertoire of visual communication concepts we have learned to make sense of the film and our responses to it. It is true, also, that the more we know of how film (or any form of visual communication) works, the more our appreciation of film is enhanced. So the more you know, the more you can appreciate forms of visual communication—or literature, music, and all other art forms.

Applications

1. Make a list of the five best films you've seen in the last year or so, ranked from one to five. What are your criteria for evaluating a film—that is, what makes a film "good"? Do you think there are criteria that should be generally accepted or are such things essentially a matter of opinion and personal taste? Compare your list with those of your classmates to see whether there is any agreement on which were the best films.

2. If you think a film is wonderful and a friend thinks the film is terrible, what is the "truth" of the matter? Is one of you likely to be correct and another likely to be incorrect, or can you both be correct? Why is taste an unreliable guide to aesthetic judgments?

3. Videotape a film, then play it without the sound for a while, so that you can concentrate on such matters as facial expression, lighting, editing, kinds of shots. Rewind it and play it with sound. Do you have a better understanding of how the film was made and how it achieves its effects?

4. What makes a film a "classic"? In what ways are "classic" films different from ordinary films?

5. Can you think of ways in which films have been influenced by television's visual techniques? Be specific about the films and the techniques.

6. Suppose you were asked to teach a course on contemporary American culture (since the 1960s). Which films would you use to give your students an understanding of our culture in all its variety? Justify your choices.

Television:
The Ever-Changing
Mosaic

Chapter 5

The Television Image

Watching television is considerably different from watching film. The film image is like a discrete photograph, loaded with information and very high in resolution. When we watch a film, we see twenty-four of these images per second; each stops for a very brief period of time and then is followed by another frame. Because of the lingering afterimage, we get the effect or, should we say, have the illusion of motion.

The television image is altogether different. It is best described as a mosaic, made up of a large quantity of dots that are constantly changing. As Marshall McLuhan put it in *Understanding Media: The Extensions of Man* (1965:313):

> With TV, the viewer is the screen. He is bombarded with light impulses that James Joyce called the "Charge of the Light Brigade" that imbues his "soulskin with sobconscious inklings." The TV image is visually low in data. The TV image is not a still shot. It is not photo in any sense, but a ceaselessly forming contour of things limned by the scanning finger . . . The TV image offers some three million dots per second to the receiver. From these he accepts only a few dozen each instant, from which to make an image.

McLuhan probably underestimated the number of dots we use to make images, but his point is correct: a television image is a constantly changing mosaic of dots, and viewers must make sense of them (Figures 5.1, 5.2, 5.3). We can do so with great facility and ease, but the point is we *must* do so.

Essentially, television is more like radio than it is different from it. As with radio, the concept of flow is all-important; the product of both media is continuous and continuing, with both the smaller unit of the show and the larger unit of the day's or evening's programming. Moreover, because of the relatively poor quality of the televised image (as compared with theatrical film), TV depends heavily on its audio component. The curved screen, the lack of definition and contrast, the difficulties of broadcast reception, all work to minimize the effectiveness of the TV image. Visually, the density of information is low, which is made up for in part by a relatively compressed density of programming and sequencing. The segue and lead-in of radio are also of prime significance in the grammar of television: dead space and dead time are to be avoided at all costs: the flow must continue. (pp. 362,363)

JAMES MONACO, *How to Read a Film*

97

It is this difference between the amount of data given by the television image and the screen image that led McLuhan to suggest that differences in media are more important than the differences in the programs or genres they carry or, as he put it, "the medium is the message." McLuhan has a highly controversial theory that distinguishes between "hot" media and "cool" media. A hot medium, he tells us in *Understanding Media* (1965:22) "is one that extends one single sense in 'high definition.' High definition is being well filled with data." When there is high definition, McLuhan adds, there is low participation. A cool medium, on the other hand, has low definition, offers relatively few data, and fosters high participation.

A list of hot and cool media, as McLuhan sees things, follows.

Hot	*Cool*
film	television
radio	telephone
photograph	cartoon
printed word	speech
lecture	seminar
book	dialogue

The television image, because it is so low in data relative to the film image, is cool and encourages (or should we say requires) participation and attention.

The very nature of the television image, then, has a significance and an impact on viewers. According to McLuhan, television is more involving than film, requires more effort from the viewer, and is used in different ways by viewers. However, studies reveal that people do not, in fact, always watch television with undiluted attention; the set is on in a lighted room and people watching it often converse with one another, eat, read, and do all kinds of things. And they watch more than three and one-half hours of television per day in America. (The TV set is on almost seven hours per day in a typical home.)

From McLuhan's perspective this is important because he believes that the medium of television has altered our sense ratios or patterns of perception and that this development has had a profound impact upon us (and people in other countries as well, since this alteration varies from culture to culture). As he writes (1965:45):

> There is . . . no way of refusing to comply with the new sense ratios of the TV image. But the effect of the entry of the TV image will vary from culture to culture in accordance with the existing sense ratios in each culture. In audio-tactile Europe TV has intensified the visual

FIGURE 5.1
Photo of television image at 1/1000 second.

FIGURE 5.2
Photo of television image at 1/500 second.

FIGURE 5.3
Photo of television image at 1/125 second.

sense, spurring them toward American styles of packaging and dressing. In America, the intensely visual culture, TV has opened the doors of audio-tactile perception to the non-visual world of spoken languages and food and the plastic arts.

McLuhan's theories were very controversial when he launched them in the early 1960s. Now they are not so frequently discussed; but they explain a good deal and, if taken with a grain of salt, help us understand why different media affect us the way they do.

The Television Screen

When we go to the movies we sit in a large room and watch huge images on a very large screen. Movie screens vary in shape — depending upon how the films are shot — but they are all large, and some are even gigantic. The television screen, on the other hand, is relatively small. Many sets have a twelve-inch screen (measured diagonally), though the most common size screen is a good deal larger than that, ranging from nineteen inches to twenty-five inches. There are even larger screens but they are much more expensive and not as widely used.

The small television screen means that images are relatively small, which is why many people argue that television is a close-up medium. As Esslin writes in *The Age of Television* (1982:30,32):

> Television is the most voyeuristic of all communication media, not only because it provides more material in an unending stream of images and in the form most universally acceptable to the total population, but also because it is the most intimate of the dramatic media. In the theatre, the actors are relatively remote from the audience, and the dramatic occasion is public. In the cinema, also a public occasion gathering a large audience into a single room, the actors are nearer to the spectators than in the theatre, but in close-ups they are larger than life. Television is seen at close range and in a more private context. *The close-up of the television performer is on a scale that most nearly approximates direct human contact.* [My italics]

Thus the close-up image on television, uniquely, gives us the illusion of being with others, which has profound psychological implications. It is television, more than any other medium, that can generate pseudo-companionship, an electronic intimacy that is illusory and not real (Figure 5.4).

From this perspective, our sense of "knowing" characters on television and our erotic feelings about them would be much

FIGURE 5.4
Lee Friedlander. The photograph reflects the fact that many people watch television from bed.

stronger than with characters from films, especially if we watch television programs that are serial in nature and expose us to these characters daily (or weekly) for extended periods of time.

The small screen also means that action on television takes place on the Z-axis, the axis that extends from the viewer through the television screen and that is perpendicular to it. On a huge film screen, action can move horizontally across the screen and not lose impact. On the tiny television set, things are different. The only way to deal with large spaces is via the Z-axis, which means action generally moves toward and away from the viewer. The viewer is therefore more directly involved in action. Figures 5.5 and 5.6 show the difference between A-B axis action and Z-axis action.

It is possible to suggest, then, that the small size of the television screen involves viewers in two ways: via the close-up, which approximates human conversational distance, and via the Z-axis, which situates the viewers so that action almost always takes place toward or away from them.

Watching a film on television is different, then, from watching the same film in a theatre. The film does not focus as directly on the viewer and the Z-axis or rely so heavily on close-ups, so that the impact of the film, when it is seen on the television screen, is different from its impact when seen in a theatre. The quality of the image is also different, and this has an effect on the film's impact. The film image, which is very powerful and full of information, is turned into a television image and thus diluted.

This does not mean we cannot get a good deal of pleasure from watching a film on television; the incredible development of the videocassette rental industry for films shows that people like to watch films on their VCR systems. But they are not having the same experience as seeing the film in a theatre, with a large screen and a powerful stereophonic audio system. (It is likely that it is the amount of money people save on tickets and baby-sitters by renting videocassettes that is of primary importance; convenience may also be a factor.)

Talking Heads

There is an element of conventional wisdom in the television industry about avoiding programs with "talking heads." If all one has is a program with no variety of camera shots and the talk from these talking heads is dull and uninteresting, the program featuring these talking heads will, indeed, be dull.

But it isn't as simple as that. Many programs that involve, for the most part, talking heads are extremely interesting and diverting. On the Public Broadcasting System, for example, two of the most popular programs—popular for many years, also—have been "Washington Week in Review" and "Wall Street Week." In the first program, a group of reporters sit around a table and talk about the news and politics and, in the second, financial advisors talk about money. There is not much in the way of action; but since the topics of these two programs—politics and money—are of great interest to large numbers of people, there doesn't have to be any action. In fact, any action would be counterproductive.

In the summer of 1987, the Iran-Contra hearings took place before joint House and Senate committees; and millions of people watched, transfixed, as a collection of incredible characters came before the cameras to tell fantastic stories about their actions and activities. These recalled the McCarthy hearings of the 1950s and the Watergate hearings of the 1970s—other occasions when millions were enthralled by "talking heads."

FIGURE 5.5
This drawing shows the A-B axis. It is a simplification of the Johnnie Walker advertisement shown in Figure 2.14.

FIGURE 5.6
This drawing shows the Z-axis. It is a simplification of the Johnnie Walker advertisement shown in Figure 2.36.

During the Iran-Contra hearings, witnesses contradicted one another and revealed amazing things about what was going on in the White House and how American foreign policy was being conducted. The hearings "created" a new American hero (at least for some people), Oliver North, whose hairstyle was promptly imitated by large numbers of young men and whose appearance also seems to have had, at least in the short run, benefits for the Contras and military recruiting.

In these hearings (and in all "talking-heads" programs), the camera played an important role and was very active—scanning the committee, zooming in on witnesses who were testifying, showing important evidence that had been enlarged and posted on the walls of the committee hearing room. An active camera can generate energy and force viewers to think in certain ways (thus, the zoom in suggests that we pay attention because something important is going on). The camera work can add an element of drama to a given program.

If one of the functions of television is to bring personalities to viewers, there's nothing in the talking head format that prevents this from being done. In the final analysis, it is the quality of the people who are talking and what they have to say that is crucial. And a great number of formats on television are little more than talking heads: quiz programs, talk shows, interview shows, and political speeches.

Television Genres

There are three kinds of programs (or genres, to use the technical term) on television that are particularly significant in terms of visual communication: the commercial, the news program, and MTV (music television). The commercial is also important because it is the cash-cow that finances television. In fact, some media critics have suggested that television programming exists to furnish an audience for the commercials, which are the most important genre carried by the medium.

We must make a distinction between a medium, such as television, and the program genres it carries: commercials, news shows, sports programs, science fiction programs, talk shows, soap operas, situation comedies, crime shows, and so on. Many critics pay little attention to the impact of a medium on a genre, which means they neglect a matter of considerable importance. It is very much an oversimplification to argue that "the program is the message" as it is to argue that "the medium is the message."

The Commercial

In 1987, advertisers spent $102 billion dollars on all media, and approximately $22 billion on television. That translates into an enormous number of commercials. As a result of the high cost of air time, commercials are getting shorter and shorter, which means they must compress their messages into thirty seconds of air time or, lately, fifteen seconds. This compression obviously has an impact on the visual aspects of the commercial.

One thing that the commercial did was to get rid of the establishing shot — the long shot that gives a viewer a sense of context. Films used establishing shots regularly. We would see an extreme long shot of a building; then the camera would pan along the street to the building, up the building to a window, into the window where the action would begin. The commercial plunges the viewers right into the middle of the action and gets them involved immediately. Films have now adopted this convention and, like commercials, now "start in the middle."

Many commercials can be described as micro-dramas, in which a traditional plot is compressed to thirty seconds. In these micro-dramas, the product is a miraculous agent that resolves problems and allows the characters to , we surmise, live happily ever after (Figure 5.7).

To sell as quickly and convincingly as possible, actors and actresses in commercials use a great deal of facial expression and body language. If you turn off the sound and just watch commercials, you can see that many of the characters really exaggerate their facial expressions and body language. The exaggeration counters the brevity of their performances and the disbelief that viewers bring to commercials. They also use their voices, all kinds of different props, their sexuality, humor, and anything else they can to convince viewers to buy a given product or service.

Analyzing the Commercial

Television exists, it has been suggested, to provide audiences for companies selling goods and services. Thus, the commercial is television's most important genre — and, in certain respects, its most interesting. Commercials cost an enormous amount of money to produce and to air, on stations and networks. The people who make commercials are some of the best and most creative individuals in the advertising and film and video world. We can learn a great deal, then, from studying these mini-dramas to see how they work and obtain their effects. What

Levi's

TITLE: "STRANGER"
COMMERCIAL NO. LZMB 7101

LENGTH: 60
PRODUCT: SLACKS and JEANS

There was this stranger who came into our town. He was tall and dark and had eyes that could look right down to the bottom of you.

We might've welcomed him to our tight little circle . . . except for one thing: his pants! They weren't dull like ours. And this troubled us.

"Stranger, how is it **your** pants have stripes? And flared legs?" He just smiled and said,

"Why, I'm wearing **Levi's**. Because dull is a downer, and not my style."

Then, in his strange way, . . .

. . . he transported us to the world of Levi's Sta-Prest slacks and jeans.

Stars . . . stripes . . .

. . . flares . . . jeans . . .

. . . colors . . . cords . . . hopsack . . . houndstooth . . . herringbone—

—It was magic! Beautiful Levi's magic. And we cried for more!

But in his quiet manner he told us, "No, I must go to other towns." And he left. Left us to our new Levi's.

Looking back, we miss that stranger. But you know, life has never been dull in our town again. By the way—how are things in **your** town?

LEVI STRAUSS & CO., 98 BATTERY ST., SAN FRANCISCO, CALIF. 94106 • TELEPHONE (415) 391-6200

FIGURE 5.7
Storyboard for Levi's commercial—"The Stranger." This storyboard shows some of the significant images found in the commercial. Since the commercial was an animated film, it was possible to show images exactly as they would be broadcast in the commercial.

follows is a list of some of the more important topics to consider in analyzing commercials. Consider the storyboard in Figure 5.7 as well as that in Figure 5.8 while you read this list.

Narrative structure What happens in the commercial? What is its plot — if a plot exists? What techniques are used to captivate the viewers? Are there flashbacks or flashforwards? Is there a narrator? Is there action? Is there conflict?

The characters Who are the characters in the commercial? What are their characteristics? What relationships seem to exist among them? Are they appealing? Are they funny? Are there hunks and glamor girls? If so, what function do they have? How are we supposed to relate to these characters? What about their faces (and use of facial expression), the style and color of their hair, the shape of their bodies, their age, the clothes they wear, the possessions they have? What kind of voices do they have? How might they help sell the product or service being advertised?

The dialogue What kind of language is used? What techniques of persuasion are used to sell viewers: humor, scare tactics and the generation of anxiety, sexuality and "seductiveness," appeals to authority, appeals to vanity, pleading, etc.

The setting Where does the action take place? When does it take place? What significance does the setting have? Are there any props of importance — furniture, paintings, machines, gadgets, cars, etc.?

The visuals What kinds of shots are found in the commercial? Is there a variety of shots: close-ups, extreme close-ups, long shots, etc.? What shot angles are used and what effect do these shot angles have?

What about the editing? How is the commercial cut? Is there hardly any cutting at all or do we find a great deal of quick cutting? If there is quick cutting, what impact does this quick cutting have? Do we find such things as dissolves, distortion, compression, fade-outs? What impact do these phenomena have?

Also, how is color used? What colors are found in the commercial and what role do these colors play? What kinds of effects are generated by the colors? How is the color related to the lighting?

The store of knowledge in the viewers What generally held beliefs, attitudes, values, ideas, myths, heroic archetypes, etc., are reflected in the commercial?

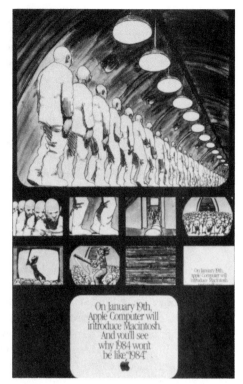

FIGURE 5.8
Storyboard for "1984" commercial by Chiat/Day Advertising, Los Angeles.

Because commercials are so compressed, they are forced to draw upon and use information and ideas their viewers already have in their heads. The primary function of the commercial is to generate a response, to create "desire," not convey information. Commercials make use of the stock of information we all have picked up, often through our experiences and the mass media, for their own purposes.

It is useful to think of commercials as "sign systems" and to consider every aspect of a commercial as a sign to be interpreted. Thus, all of the topics discussed in this book can be used to interpret and understand the fascinating (and often irritating) art form we know as the commercial.

Television News

News programs (documentaries and certain videos) are at the opposite end of the disbelief spectrum. Numerous surveys indicate that large numbers of Americans get most of their news from television news programs and think that the news shows are more believable than stories in newspapers, for example. We know, however, that while the camera doesn't lie, the person who controls the camera can "lie" or, at least, determine what is presented to the viewing public.

In a famous study of a parade in Chicago for General Douglas MacArthur after he had been fired by President Truman, Kurt and Gladys Engel Lang showed that what was presented on television news programs was quite different from what really went on. The actual parade was a rather dull affair and not too many people were there; but, by using only certain shots, the television news directors led viewers to believe that it was an exciting event with mobs of people. As we saw in the discussion of photography, cameras don't lie but liars use cameras.

News programs are also interesting for those interested in visual communications because they use a large number of graphics, captions, and similar phenomena. Even though television news is visual and aural, there is still need for the written word and for various kinds of signs, charts, and graphs. These are necessary because they can show relationships very well and compress a great deal of complex information into a relatively simple visual display. The news program (at least the national news) is generally a very sober affair that strives for realism. But events on news programs are often dramatized so that they are entertainments as well.

Checklist for Analyzing Television Commercials

1. Narrative Structure
   a. What happens?
   b. What dramatic techniques are used?
   c. Is there a narrator? What is the narrator's function?
   d. Is there action? What significance does it have?
   e. Is there conflict? How is it resolved?

2. The Characters
   a. Who are they? What roles do they play?
   b. What do they look like? Facial features, hair color, body types?
   c. What relationship seems to exist among them?
   d. What are their demographics: age, sex, race, etc.?
   e. What are their voices like?
   f. How do they help sell the product or service?

3. The Dialogue
   a. What kind of language is used?
   b. What techniques of persuasion are used?
   c. What rhetorical techniques are used?

4. The Setting
   a. Where does the action take place?
   b. What significance does the setting have?
   c. Are any props of importance used?

5. The Visuals
   a. What kind of shots are used?
   b. How is the commercial edited?
   c. How is color used?
   d. How is lighting used?

6. The Viewers
   a. How does the commercial use information the viewers have?
   b. How does the commercial relate to popularly held beliefs, myths, ideas, attitudes, values, and archetypes.

In other words, the producer of a news program can make the news "exciting" by injecting dramatic elements into stories — who is winning or losing, who is lying or telling the truth, or what important consequences will stem from a given event. Visually, national newscasts all have a similar look: we see the anchor or anchors sitting at a desk with screens in the background. The anchor narrates the news and the program switches back and forth between the anchor and the field reporters, who are usually shown on the screens, interviewing important figures or showing some scene that is of consequence.

Because television is a visual medium, many critics have suggested that television news focuses on stories that have a visual dimension to them and neglect many important stories that don't. Whatever the case, the national news is on for approximately twenty-four minutes (the other six minutes are taken up with commercials), and it cannot go into great depth for any story, which is why some media analysts have suggested that television news is essentially a headline service. If you want details, background, and analysis, you have to go to a print medium, such as a newspaper or magazine (or to a program like "The MacNeil-Lehrer News Hour" on public television).

Music Television (MTV)

This genre is particularly interesting for students of visual communication because we find that MTV has a particular look to it. The music videos broadcast on television are, in fact, commercials for records that are produced by various musical groups. Depending upon how much money was available and the artistic inclinations of the producer, the videos generally either show the band making the song or turn the song into some kind of a dramatic piece.

What is interesting about music videos is that so many of them have surrealistic qualities. Surrealism is a visual style that is dreamlike, nonlinear (full of flashforwards and flashbacks), makes use of fantastic images and distorted perspectives, and is full of special effects (Figures 5.9, 5.10, 5.11). The term *surrealism* comes from painting and describes a group of highly experimental artists such as Miro, Dali, Breton, and Magritte who worked in the 1920s (and later) and who wanted to represent the unconscious mind with their paintings.

We find surrealistic elements in many music videos, a surprising combination of avant-garde visual aesthetics and rather ordinary, formulaic musical aesthetics. One of the problems with

FIGURE 5.9
Lynn Hershman, still from "Lorna," 1984.
This still shows the use of typographic print
images superimposed over extreme close-up
of lips.

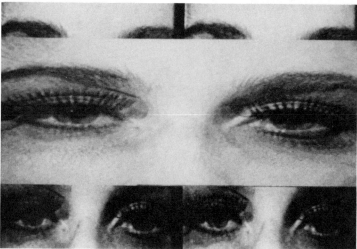

FIGURE 5.10
Lynn Hershman, still from "Eyewitness,"
1984. This image has surrealistic elements in
its use of various pairs of eyes.

music television is that after watching it for an hour or so, it tends
to blur in your mind. There's been so much visual excitement
that you suffer from a bad case of "information overload."

These music videos, one might argue, take the experimental-
ism and vitality found in the commercial and push these phenomena to their furthest limits. They have, in turn, greatly influenced the look of regular commercials and also have impacted
on the psyches of the teenagers (and others) who watch them.

FIGURE 5.11
Lynn Hershman, still from "Birdie," 1987.
This surrealistic image was created using a
Proteus computer.

Video Artists

It is hard, at times, to know where to draw the line between what we call commercial television and video art. The video artists, like all artists, have their private visions and use the medium of video to make personal statements, to create videos that they think are beautiful and thought-provoking. Unlike commercial television, these videos are not meant to please the general public, though videos sometimes are shown on television stations (generally public television). They are often highly imaginative, experimental in form (in the way they manipulate images, color, music, and narrative structure), and frequently have sociological and ideological dimensions to them.

Ironically, music television and other television borrows from these video artists—in the same way that the surrealists influenced other artists and impacted upon other media. The moral is that art styles and movements have an impact and influence that is quite widespread.

Flipping

The final irony, relative to the television image, stems from the development of the remote-control channel switcher. Increasingly large numbers of people use these channel switchers for "flipping," a process in which they jump, back and forth, from channel to channel. Estimates suggest that about a third of television watchers flip regularly and more than 50 percent of teenagers do so.

What this means is that people are not so much watching television programs as television itself. (This is a big problem for advertising agencies who are selling audiences to advertisers. If people flip at the first sign of a commercial, or even before that, the whole television advertising industry is in trouble.) Not only is the television screen a mosaic, but people are also turning television itself into a kind of mosaic and simultaneously watching (to the extent the term *watching* applies) a dozen or more television programs at the same time.

This reduces television to its elemental form — visual images — and people who flip essentially turn television into a set of visual images (and auditory stimuli) at the expense of program form and continuity. We have a micro-mosaic reaching its audience in the form of what we might call macro-mosaic, a huge surrealistic collection of bits and pieces of many different programs and stories that become a person's television program. People who flip make their own television programs out of the programming available at a given time — an electronic montage. Thanks to the remote-control device, we can all become video artists.

Conclusions

Television is the medium everyone loves to hate. It has been described as a "vast wasteland" and is the object of endless condemnation by elitists, many of whom take pride in never watching it. It is also the object of countless studies by psychologists, sociologists, and other social scientists, who investigate its effect on everything from our family lives to our sex lives, not to mention our political behavior.

One of the most important shortcomings of many studies of television is that they pay no attention to the visual and aesthetic aspects of the medium. The basic model for most studies comes from social psychology and is concerned with the impact of television on attitudes, beliefs, and values — which can then be used to predict everything from consumer behavior to voting behavior. This model, which neglects the power of images, sound, and other aesthetic factors (such as the kinds of shots used, the cutting, etc.), is simplistic and not adequate to deal with television in all of its complexity.

Fortunately, this emphasis is changing; and as interest in visual communication progresses, it is hoped that new and better ways of studying television will emerge.

Applications

1. Watch commercials without the sound so that you can pay attention to their technical aspects. What do you find of interest?

2. Assume you are asked to create a commercial for some product. Create a storyboard for the projected commercial (with six or eight frames) and be prepared to explain to a potential client why you did what you did. How will your commercial help sell the product?

3. Create a new television genre by mixing various television genres and write a one-paragraph description of the show, for newspapers, that would describe the show for potential viewers. You can use up to three genres.

4. Tape three network news programs and compare them in terms of the order of topics, the topics covered, and related concerns. Are there important similarities? If so, why? Are there important differences? If so, how do you explain this? (You can do the same for local news programs also. See if you can figure out how the show with the highest ratings differs from its competitors.)

5. Make a list of the topics covered in a network news program and compare it with the first page of the *New York Times*. What do you find? Is television news just a "headline" service? What does that mean?

6. Using everything you've learned about visual communication, analyze a music video that you find interesting. Consider such matters as: the images, the cutting, the lighting, the use of color, the way performers are shot, the way women are shown (and their roles), the way men are shown (and their roles), the lyrics, and anything else that you think is of interest. Why has music video been so successful?

Comics and Cartoons

Chapter 6

The Comic Strip

Comic strips have been prominent features of American newspapers since the early 1900s, and some media scholars have suggested that, in many respects, the comic strip is an American idiom. Describing the comic strip as an American medium would be more proper. We created a huge number of comic strips, many of which we now look upon as "classics" and are now beginning to reprint in huge art books.

We now see that the comic strip has an aesthetic quality of its own and that the strips are important repositories of our values and beliefs. For this reason, historians and sociologists have made increasing use of the comics as a kind of documentary record of American culture—especially in the early part of the twentieth century. Many comic strips lasted fifty or sixty years; in some cases a strip has been kept going after the original artist died by bringing in a different artist. This is the case with *Blondie*, which started in 1930 and still is being published.

Reading the Comics

A comic strip can be defined as a form of pictorial art that has the following attributes:

1. Continuing characters
2. Frames that show the action
3. Dialogue in balloons (generally speaking)

Normal dialogue appears in balloons with an unbroken outline, with the tail pointing to the speaker. A perforated line indicates whispering. If the words are written in very small letters within a big balloon, it means the speaker is astonished or ashamed. A cry has a spiky outline, and the famous "telephone voice" has a zig-zag shape, with a zig-zag arrow disappearing into the telephone. Balloons indicating cold or conceited voices have little icicles sprouting from their undersides. Thought balloons are connected with the thinker by a series of little circles which look like bubbles, and if a speech balloon has a little arrow pointing outside the picture, the speaker is "off."

RHEINHOLD REITBERGER AND WOLFGANG FUCHS, *Comics: Anatomy of a Mass Medium*

Although we call them "comics" or "the funnies," there are many comic strips that are serious—so the term is really misleading. (The French use the term "designed bands" which does not imply that all comics are humorous.) Many of our greatest comic strips—*Dick Tracy, Little Orphan Annie, Buck Rogers, Tarzan*—are not funny.

We can make a distinction between comics and cartoons: cartoons do not have continuing characters and do not have dialogue shown in balloons. And some cartoons, political ones, are not funny or meant to make people laugh.

There are, it turns out, a number of conventions we have to learn if we are to read the comics correctly. Let's look at them.

The way characters are drawn In some comics, the style is realistic and in others it is highly stylized and meant to be funny. These characters have big noses, big ears, silly looks on their faces, and so on. We learn from the way the characters are drawn how to classify the strip—as funny or as serious.

Facial expression Being a visual art, comics make considerable use of facial expression to show the feelings or emotional states of the various characters. Exaggerated facial expression is one way comic strip artists can inject humor into their strips.

The role of balloons Comic strip artists use various methods to let us know how to respond to the dialogue of the characters. Sometimes the words are shown in heavy print or in some other typeface. We often find exclamation marks used. There is another convention that is important here: thoughts are shown in scalloped balloons, and so comic strip artists can show what people are saying and thinking by using different kinds of balloons. Sound effects are often shown in zig-zagged balloons, to give the artists one more way of generating effects.

Movement lines Artists show movement and speed by using lines that indicate movement, and sometimes puffs of smoke to show how fast someone or something is moving.

Panels at the bottom or top of the frame These panels are used for continuity and to tell the reader what to expect or what is going on at a given moment.

The setting A given setting provides readers with a sense of what is going on and how seriously one is to take things.

The action   Each frame in a comic strip is the equivalent of a frame in a film, except that dialogue is shown in the comic strip, thoughts are revealed, and narration is provided through the printed word. The comic strip provides points of action that readers must fill in or complete in their own minds — this is quite similar to the "jump cut" of film.

Comic strips are often collaborations between writers and artists, though the old humorous comic strips were generally drawn and written by the same person. The artists who draw these strips use a variety of different kinds of shots and shot angles in telling their stories. The artists must be mindful of the strip or the page (in the case of comic books) and make certain that they maintain visual interest by varying the kinds of shots and shot angles. (In this respect, the storyboards used in planning television commercials are very much like comic books: the storyboards show six or eight basic shots and indicate the dialogue that goes with each shot.)

As we grow up and become accustomed to reading the comics, we learn the various conventions connected with this medium. As with film, you have to learn how to "read" comics to be able to understand them fully.

The Power of the Comic Strip

Why is this simple medium so powerful? For one thing, we spend many years with comic strips and their characters. *Peanuts,* for example, started in 1950 (Figure 6.1), and so there are many people in America who have been following that strip for close to forty years. The more we follow the strip, the more significance various events that happen in it have for us, since these events relate to the characters and their personalities and we have been observing both for long periods of time. The comic strip is an iterative medium or "art form" as some put it — the more we follow it, the more it means to us, until finally, as in the case of *Peanuts,* its characters merge into our folklore and, in a curious way, into our lives.

So the comic strip (or certain ones, at least) involve us for long periods of time, even though we may read a given episode in a matter of seconds. In addition, the comic strip has the power to create fantastic and fascinating personalities, with whom we become "involved." In certain humorous ones, we find personalities who spend decades "locked" in comedic combat with one another. Let me cite a few of these: Beetle Bailey and Sarge in *Beetle Bailey,* Krazy Kat and Offissa Pupp in *Krazy Kat,* and The Spook and the Jailors, etc., in *The Wizard of Id.*

Reprinted with permission of USF, Inc.

Reprinted with permission of USF, Inc.

Reprinted with permission of USF, Inc.

The great characters in comic strips develop their personalities over the years and we develop attachments to these characters and expectations about them. Think of *Doonesbury* (Figure 6.2) and its remarkable cast of characters who keep appearing and reappearing in various guises and situations. Garry Trudeau, *Doonesbury's* creator, has used the Max Headroom character from television (to poke fun at Ronald Reagan) with great effectiveness, an excellent example of intertextuality.

FIGURE 6.1
The evolution of drawing style in Charles Shulz's *Peanuts.*

The remarkable capacity of the comic strip to generate memorable characters is another reason why comics are so powerful. We continually search for personalities with whom we can identify (and to whom we can relate, even if only through a medium), and so the comic strip, which can generate personalities who have extraordinarily long lives (as fictional characters go) has much more impact on people than we might imagine.

In addition, the art style of some cartoons is extremely expressive and often quite individualistic, and the use of grotesques (visually and psychologically) gives the comic strip a unique power. A French scholar even wrote a book, *Black and White in the Comics,* which deals with the visual attributes of the comic strip. The grotesque is an art style that uses exaggerated and often distorted physical characteristics to make a point. The physical ugliness of grotesques is often allied, especially in the work of Chester Gould, with their moral ugliness and criminality. Indeed, Gould created a veritable bestiary of criminal characters such as Flat Top and the Mole with whom he peopled his strip (Figure 6.3).

Psychologically, comics are filled with "grotesques" in the sense that we find numerous monomaniacs, obsessives, and single-minded types—who live only for the next meal, to escape from prison, to harass some character or whatever. Most of these grotesques are found in humorous strips where their obsessive quality becomes humorous and makes possible humor based on frustrating them. In some cases, we have momentary monomania—as in *Peanuts* where we have Lucy being congenitally unable to catch fly balls, where readers spend years watching Lucy snatch the football away just before it is kicked by Charlie Brown.

FIGURE 6.2
Garry Trudeau, *Doonesbury.* This comic strip is so political that some newspapers run it on the editorial page. Trudeau pokes fun at American social, cultural, and political fads and foibles. *Doonesbury* © 1980 G.B. Trudeau. Reprinted with permission of Universal Press Syndicate. All rights reserved.

Doonesbury

BY GARRY TRUDEAU

Cartoons

A cartoon is usually confined to one frame and does not have continuous characters though it may use certain types over and over again (or in the case of political cartoons, which are often not meant to be funny, certain political figures). The cartoon does not make use of balloons but uses captions underneath the frame to make its point. There are two types of cartoons: humorous cartoons (Figures 6.4 and 6.5), which often satirize conventions in a given society as well as certain character types, and political cartoons (Figures 6.6, 6.7, and 6.8) which make a point about some political situation and which may or may not be funny.

FIGURE 6.3
Chester Gould, *Dick Tracy*. This was one of the classic American strips, which featured a variety of grotesque-looking monster criminals. These frames from Gilbert Shelton's *Tricky Prickears* parody *Dick Tracy*.

THE FAR SIDE By GARY LARSON

FIGURE 6.4
Gary Larson, *The Far Side.* Larson is a comic genius whose offbeat sense of humor has become very popular. *The Far Side* © 1988 Universal Press Syndicate. All rights reserved.

FIGURE 6.5
Detail of cartoon from Gallo advertisement. This shows how artists can use cartoons to create arresting and amusing images.

Good heavens, Monsieur Dupont!
We didn't <u>mean</u> to win!
Honest!
Monsieur Dupont?
    Thank goodness you're feeling better! We owe you some explanation.

European grape varieties.
    We imported oak from France and Yugoslavia, to make one of the world's finest aging cellars.
    And we introduced a line of new varietal wines that have pleased the harshest of critics.

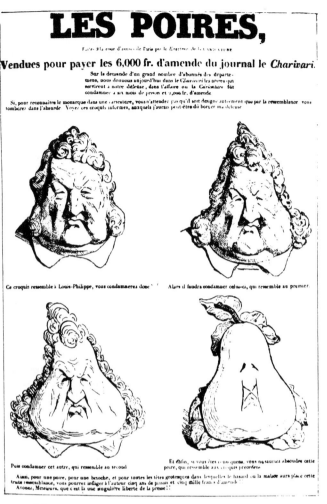

L. C. Gregg in the Atlanta *Constitution*.

FOR PRESIDENT!

FIGURE 6.7
L. C. Gregg, "For President," circa 1904,
Atlanta Constitution. This political cartoon is
an optical illusion in which Teddy
Roosevelt's image was created by using
various objects, a technique used many
centuries earlier by the Italian artist
Arcimboldo. The objects are all connected
with militarism, death, and war and
generate a negative impression of Roosevelt.

FIGURE 6.6
Philipon, "The Pears," *Le Charivari*, January 17, 1831. The artist
used the image of a pear, playing upon his face and physique, to
caricature France's King Louis-Philippe. Censors of the king
eventually forbade artists to draw any pear-like figures.

The cartoon often relies heavily upon information known to
the reader and thus functions by striking a responsive chord —
by making us see something we didn't see before or recognize
the cupidity and stupidity of humans, animals, and our institutions. Cartoonists often develop a "line" or style that makes
them recognizable and a stance or point of view, as well.

Many of the common techniques of humor are available to the cartoonist — who can set characters up and manipulate them for comic effect. Cartoonists use techniques such as revelation of ignorance, mistakes, exaggeration, coincidence, satire, parody, and reversals. Therefore, although the elements of the cartoon are rather simple, the possibilities for expression are almost limitless.

FIGURE 6.8
Oliphant is recognized as one of the great political cartoonists of the time. His ability to caricature figures and his biting wit lead to many memorable cartoons. *Oliphant* © 1988 Universal Press Syndicate. Reprinted with permission. All rights reserved.

Visual Humor in Cartoons

A number of important techniques of visual humor can be used in cartoons:

Exaggeration Here the artist makes funny drawings in which feet are very large, noses are elongated, bodies are very large (relative to the size of heads or just in general), ears stick out, and so on. Exaggeration is a standard technique used by humorists; in this case, the exaggeration is physical — and may reflect the zany psychological characteristics of the characters.

Caricature This is a form of portraiture in which a character's likeness is preserved but great liberties are taken with his or her face (Figure 6.9). This technique is often used in political cartoons to ridicule a person. Often, the person portrayed is also made fun of by being put into some embarrassing situation — usually of political or social significance, frequently very negative and unflattering in nature.

We should not underestimate the power of caricature. It is commonly held that a famous political figure, Boss Tweed, was destroyed by the caricatures of a political cartoonist, Thomas Nast, in the early 1870s. Many brilliant political cartoonists are currently syndicated, and their work appears in many newspapers (Figure 6.10).

Mistakes Here we find characters misunderstanding gestures or making other mistakes that have a visual dimension to them. This kind of humor may be described as humor of identity: it involves something problematical with identity, as in the case of a dog begging in front of a statue of a man who seems to be holding something to eat or a porcupine mistaking a cactus for another porcupine and saying to it, "I love you."

FIGURE 6.9
John Updike, *Caricature of Art Berger*, circa 1954. This caricature was drawn by the author John Updike. Note the simplicity of the drawing and the way Updike exaggerates the features of the subject. Compare the caricature with the photograph of the subject to see what the caricaturist has seized on to emphasize in his drawing.

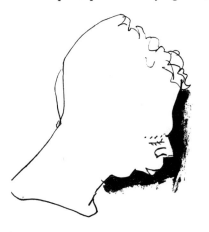

FIGURE 6.10
Thomas Nast, "A Group of Vultures
Waiting for the Storm to 'Blow Over' —Let
Us Prey," wood engraving, *Harper's Weekly*,
September 23, 1871. Nast's savage cartoons
played a major role in bringing down the
notorious "Boss Tweed." His turning
Tweed into a vulture is a typical device of
caricaturists.

Visual puns Here we take a linguistic pun and play with it and
generate visual puns to go along with it. I have, for example,
taken the word *con* (as in convict) and drawn a number of visual
puns based on the term: content, concave, and so on. These puns
use the cartoon convention of the convict as a person in striped
clothing and sometimes chained to a huge iron ball as a point of
departure (Figure 6.11).

FIGURE 6.11
Arthur Asa Berger, "CONS." These drawings are visual puns that play with sounds and meanings. What are these "cons"? See page 128 for answers.

Comic illustrations Here we find a drawing that comments on, or relates somehow (often quite indirectly) in a funny way, to something in the text. The secret is to visualize a drawing or cartoon that people will connect with the content of the text. *The Journal of Communication* is one periodical that uses such cartoons; an example is shown in Figure 6.12.

Humorous allusions Here the artist plays upon certain historical, legendary, or mythological figures or events in the public's mind for comic effect, essentially by parodying them. Heroes and heroines from films, famous works of fiction, or the comics, can also be used. This technique is often used in political cartoons, where a politician is shown as a would-be Superman or a Greek god or some other figure, except that the drawing pokes fun at the person (who is also caricatured). In some cases, the cartoonists use "types" of persons or characters, such as the Huns or wimps or zanies of one sort or another. There is an unflattering connection made (or comparison) between the figure and the type portrayed (Figure 6.13).

The cartoon, then, by utilizing our collective consciousness and various techniques of visual comedy, is a powerful and popular art form.

FIGURE 6.12
Arthur Asa Berger, "The Secret Agent," *Journal of Communication,* 1974. This is a self-caricature that appeared in an article in which the author/artist tried to explain how he worked and used the analogy of the professor/pop culturist as "secret agent."

Culture and the Comics

The elements in comic strips and cartoons may be relatively simple—line drawings and words, for the most part—but the impact of these art forms can be quite strong. We now recognize that seemingly simple phenomena can trigger powerful emotional responses in people, because these phenomena (the sound of rain, a symbol, a kind of lighting) are often connected to profoundly important experiences people have had, which are stored in their memories and called to mind, somehow, by something in the comic strip or cartoon—just as they are by verbal or visual images in "classic" literature or art.

The pictorial arts have a long history—from drawings by cavemen on the walls of caves, thousands and thousands of years ago, to the latest episode of *Peanuts* or *The Far Side* found in the morning newspaper. There is a kind of magic and power to capturing an image that we have recognized and made use of—for millennia, it would seem. Some scholars have suggested that precursors of the comic book appeared centuries ago, and we know that the political cartoon has a history hundreds of years old.

One reason the comic book and cartoon have been so popular is that they are extremely flexible and can be used for a variety of purposes. For example, the U.S. Army has found that it is helpful to use the comic book format in teaching soldiers how to use and maintain some equipment. And many people use a form of cartoon—greeting cards—to express emotions indirectly, especially emotions that they find it hard to communicate directly (Figure 6.14).

Comics and cartoons also can be used for advertising; the comic strip simulates action and has the power of the storyboard,

FIGURE 6.13
Detail of cartoon in Henry Weinhard beer advertisement. Note the use of exaggeration in creating this amusing image.

FIGURE 6.14
Chris Van Dusen, "Happy Birthday, Mom."

which is used in designing commercials. From McLuhan's point of view, the storyboard, having less information than the commercial, would generate stronger involvement on the part of readers than would the commercial itself.

And we all have seen how the comic strip has evolved into the animated film, which is a remarkable medium that can generate very powerful experiences. The early animated films were simple and funny; but as animation has developed, it has led to what might be described as serious animated films that use the power of the artist to create incredible characters, scenes, and events. The animated film makes possible a style called "the fantastic" and expands our horizons immeasurably.

Finally, there is the matter of the power comic strips and cartoons have to generate humor (Figure 6.15). Humor is a great enigma to man; our philosophers and scientists have been fascinated by it all through history and many of our greatest minds,

(A)

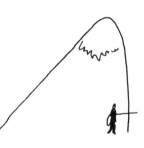

(B)

FIGURE 6.15
Arthur Asa Berger, selections from "Nosology." Here the author plays with "noses" (and sounds related to them) to create a zany kind of quiz. The title spoofs the medical term *nosology*. What are these "noses"? Here are some hints. (A) He thinks noses may not exist. (B) A disease of adolescence. (C) He has a taste for blood. (D) He had a way with words, but women scorned him. See page 128 for answers.

(C)

(D)

from Aristotle to Sigmund Freud, have tried to explain what humor is and what functions it has for people. Cartoons and comics usually generate a smile or two, rather than laughter — but this smile is a signifier of some kind of a humorous message that has been received and understood. How this happens is still a considerable mystery. We know what techniques the cartoonists and comic strip artists and writers use, but we do not know why pictorial humor makes us laugh.

Conclusions

The fact that many comic strips and comic books were funny led people to underestimate their significance, since people often assume that things that are funny (or not serious) do not have the same status as so-called serious works. We no longer make this mistake, and now many scholars and researchers are studying humor, in all of its manifestations, and granting it great importance. We have discovered that humor has important psychological, sociological, political, and even physiological significance. Humor stimulates the heart and produces various kinds of relaxation effects.

It is worth noting, then, that some of our greatest humorists are our comic strip artists and cartoonists. And in the same vein, some of our most significant — in terms of their impact upon the general public — creative artists have been our comic strip and comic book creators and our cartoonists.

Applications

1. Assume you get a job at a company that creates comic books. Create a comic book superhero or superheroine and draw the cover. How will you make your character different? Interesting? Use colors and make your drawing the size of comic books (7 by 10 inches).

2. Create an origin tale, two pages long, for your character. (The origin tale of *Superman* is two pages long.) Be sure to use all the conventions of the comic book: frames, dialogue, action, etc.

3. Make a content analysis of the comics page of your local newspaper. Do the following: count the number of frames, count the number of words spoken by male, female (and other characters), count the number of times you see male and female figures, classify the strips in some manner and list the

topics discussed or alluded to. What do the comics (or, at least the ones you've studied) reflect about American society and culture? Are any groups underrepresented? Or not represented at all?

4. Try drawing caricatures of your friends. You might find profiles are easiest, but you can try full face or three-quarter face if you wish. Try to capture their likenesses and, at the same time, exaggerate their features.

5. Using a mirror, try drawing full-face caricatures of yourself. Which features will you exaggerate? Does this exercise make you see yourself in a new light?

6. Using your skill as a caricaturist, try drawing a political cartoon. You can use the work of political cartoonists as models to imitate but the idea for the cartoon should be your own.

Answers:

"CONS" (left to right)
    Second baseman
    Concave
    Content
    Condor

    A.   Agnosetic
    B.   Monosenucleosis
    C.   Noseferatu (See page 82)
    D.   Cyranose de Bergerac

Typography and
Graphic Design

Chapter 7

Typography

Typography is, for our purposes, the art of selecting and arranging type or—in broader terms—using type in various graphic designs to obtain particular effects. Whenever you see any printed matter, the typefaces in which that material is set are based on someone's decision about which typefaces to use, how wide the margins should be, and so on. In the case of print advertisements, the decision is made by a specialist in type or, in some cases, by the art director in an agency.

Typefaces vary greatly—they have different looks about them and different meanings for people. Certain typefaces are very formal and elegant; others are casual and relaxed. Some typefaces suggest antiquity and others are very modern. The point is that just as the size of the television screen affects television programs, so do the typefaces chosen affect how people will interpret a given message. The typeface is the medium and the words set into print are the message, to recall McLuhan's ideas. The evocative power of different typefaces is particularly important in advertising, though it also affects the way we react to books and periodicals.

Types, like all of printing, are tools in communication. Printing puts information into someone's hands, influences him to feel or think a certain way, or prompts him to take or refrain from taking a certain action. The typeface is the trigger part of that tool, so to speak, because it determines the way the message looks to the reader—pleasant, pretty, messy, painful or threatening— and this in turn affects the reader's reaction to the printed message.

J. BEN LIEBERMAN, *Types of Typefaces*

129

Ever since Gutenberg developed movable type in 1440 and revolutionized the world, by making books available to the masses (ultimately, when printing became widespread), typographers have been developing different typefaces and artists have been experimenting with graphic design.

Type

We describe the size of type in points and picas, not inches. There are 12 points to a pica and approximately 6 picas to an inch. Thus we talk about 10-point type or 12-point type. Then there is the matter of the design of the letters involving matters such as:

basic shape	proportion of the parts
stance (lean)	weight or blackness
dimensions	contrast among parts
size of letter	contour or outline
width of letter	alignment along reading line
quality of line	kinds of strokes

In addition to these elements, there are many ways of classifying and describing typefaces (and there are, it is estimated, thousands of typefaces currently being used). Some of these classifications are discussed in the following sections. Generally speaking, we make distinctions between text faces and display faces.

Text typefaces   These faces are designed to be easy to read and are used for text in books, magazines, newspapers, and other media.

Display typefaces   These faces are used to generate a graphic idea or attitude and are very suggestive. They catch our attention and give personality to the messages they convey.

We also make distinctions between type faces with serifs and those without them.

Serif typefaces   A serif is a short cross-line found at the ends of letters. They were originally used in stone-cut Roman capital letters as a means of finishing off a stroke. There are variations in the size and shape of serifs, but serif faces are a general category. Some typographers believe that serif faces are easier to read than sans serif faces because serifs help tie the letters of a word together. This book is set in Palatino, a serif typeface.

Sans serif typefaces   These faces do not have serifs and have a cleaner, more contemporary look about them than serif typefaces. Figure 7.1 shows an example of a sans serif typeface.

Old English or Gothic typefaces   These faces are similar to the one used by Gutenberg in printing his Bible. He developed it out of the manuscript letter style used by scribes. It is beautiful but very difficult to read for long periods of time.

Roman typefaces   These faces were developed in the fifteenth century and were modeled after the writing styles of Roman scribes. These faces developed into three classes: Old Style, with somewhat rounded serifs and little variation in line thickness; Transitional, with more open letters and rounded serifs (such as Baskerville); and Modern, with more contrast between thick and thin lines and thin, straight serifs (such as Bodoni). Figure 7.2 gives examples of some typefaces and Figure 7.3 shows characteristics of the different classes.

Important descriptive aspects of type are discussed in the following sections.

Light and bold typefaces   A given type family often comes in many different weights—as far as the thickness of the lines is concerned. Thus we have bold faces, which are heavier and

FIGURE 7.1
Act II of Verdi's *Aida*, "the banks of the Nile, outside the Temple of Isis," as seen in the San Francisco Opera's 1984 Summer Season production. Note the supertitle, in a sans serif face, on the screen at the top of the photograph. The sans serif face was used because of its readability and because it also offers a contemporary look. These supertitles have revolutionized opera productions and have made it possible for American audiences to know what is happening in operas in considerably more detail than before.

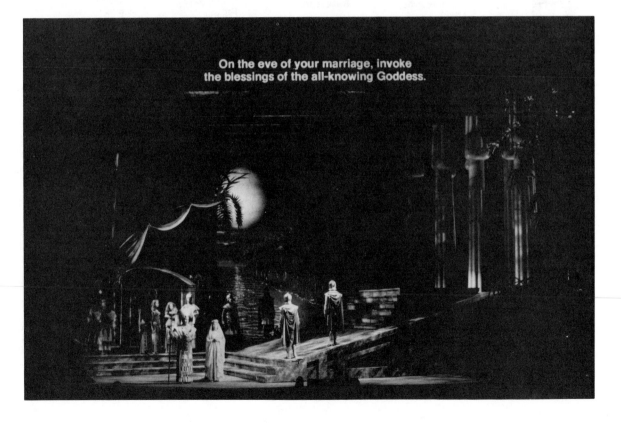

b c e

NEW FROM ITC

ITC Tiepolo™
Book
Book Italic
Bold
Bold Italic
Black
Black Italic

a

ITC American Typewriter®
Light
Medium
Bold
Light Condensed
Medium Condensed
Bold Condensed

ITC Avant Garde Gothic®
Extra Light
Extra Light Oblique
Book
Book Oblique
Medium
Medium Oblique
Demi
Demi Oblique
Bold
Bold Oblique
Book Condensed
Medium Condensed
Demi Condensed
Bold Condensed

ITC Barcelona®
Book
Book Italic
Medium
Medium Italic
Bold
Bold Italic
Heavy
Heavy Italic

ITC Bauhaus®
Light
Medium
Demi
Bold

ITC Benguiat®
Book
Book Italic
Medium
Medium Italic
Bold
Bold Italic
Book Condensed
Book Condensed Italic
Medium Condensed
Medium Condensed Italic
Bold Condensed
Bold Condensed Italic

ITC Benguiat Gothic®
Book
Book Italic
Medium
Medium Italic
Bold
Bold Italic
Heavy
Heavy Italic

ITC Berkeley Oldstyle®
Book
Book Italic
Medium
Medium Italic
Bold
Bold Italic
Black
Black Italic

ITC Bookman®
Light
Light Italic
Medium
Medium Italic
Demi
Demi Italic
Bold
Bold Italic

ITC Caslon No. 224®
Book
Book Italic
Medium
Medium Italic
Bold
Bold Italic
Black
Black Italic

ITC Century®
Light
Light Italic
Book
Book Italic
Bold
Bold Italic
Ultra
Ultra Italic
Light Condensed
Light Condensed Italic
Book Condensed
Book Condensed Italic
Bold Condensed
Bold Condensed Italic
Ultra Condensed
Ultra Condensed Italic

ITC Cheltenham®
Light
Light Italic
Book
Book Italic
Bold
Bold Italic
Ultra
Ultra Italic
Light Condensed
Light Condensed Italic
Book Condensed
Book Condensed Italic
Bold Condensed
Bold Condensed Italic
Ultra Condensed
Ultra Condensed Italic

ITC Clearface®
Regular
Regular Italic
Bold
Bold Italic
Heavy
Heavy Italic
Black
Black Italic

ITC Cushing®
Book
Book Italic
Medium
Medium Italic
Bold
Bold Italic
Heavy
Heavy Italic

ITC Élan™
Book
Book Italic
Medium
Medium Italic
Bold
Bold Italic
Black
Black Italic

ITC Eras®
Light
Book
Medium
Demi
Bold
Ultra

ITC Esprit™
Book
Book Italic
Medium
Medium Italic
Bold
Bold Italic
Black
Black Italic

ITC Fenice®
Light
Light Italic
Regular
Regular Italic
Bold
Bold Italic
Ultra
Ultra Italic

ITC Franklin Gothic®
Book
Book Italic
Medium
Medium Italic
Demi
Demi Italic
Heavy
Heavy Italic

Friz Quadrata
Friz Quadrata
Friz Quadrata Bold

ITC Galliard®
Roman
Roman Italic
Bold
Bold Italic
Black
Black Italic
Ultra
Ultra Italic

FIGURE 7.2
Examples of typefaces.

g

ITC Gamma™
Book
Book Italic
Medium
Medium Italic
Bold
Bold Italic
Black
Black Italic

ITC Garamond®
Light
Light Italic
Book
Book Italic
Bold
Bold Italic
Ultra
Ultra Italic
Light Condensed
Light Condensed Italic
Book Condensed
Book Condensed Italic
Bold Condensed
Bold Condensed Italic
Ultra Condensed
Ultra Condensed Italic

ITC Goudy Sans™
Book
Book Italic
Medium
Medium Italic
Bold
Bold Italic
Black
Black Italic

ITC Isbell®
Book
Book Italic
Medium
Medium Italic
Bold
Bold Italic
Heavy
Heavy Italic

Italia
Book
Medium
Bold

k

ITC Kabel®
Book
Medium
Demi
Bold
Ultra

ITC Korinna®
Regular
Kursiv Regular
Bold
Kursiv Bold
Extra Bold
Kursiv Extra Bold
Heavy
Kursiv Heavy

ITC Leawood®
Book
Book Italic
Medium
Medium Italic
Bold
Bold Italic
Black
Black Italic

ITC Lubalin Graph®
Extra Light
Extra Light Oblique
Book
Book Oblique
Medium
Medium Oblique
Demi
Demi Oblique
Bold
Bold Oblique

ITC Mixage®
Book
Book Italic
Medium
Medium Italic
Bold
Bold Italic
Black
Black Italic

m

ITC Modern No. 216®
Light
Light Italic
Medium
Medium Italic
Bold
Bold Italic
Heavy
Heavy Italic

ITC New Baskerville®
Roman
Italic
Semi Bold
Semi Bold Italic
Bold
Bold Italic
Black
Black Italic

ITC Newtext®
Light
Light Italic
Book
Book Italic
Regular
Regular Italic
Demi
Demi Italic

ITC Novarese®
Book
Book Italic
Medium
Medium Italic
Bold
Bold Italic
Ultra

ITC Pacella™
Book
Book Italic
Medium
Medium Italic
Bold
Bold Italic
Black
Black Italic

ITC Quorum®
Light
Book
Medium
Bold
Black

S

ITC Serif Gothic®
Light
Regular
Bold
Extra Bold
Heavy
Black

ITC Slimbach™
Book
Book Italic
Medium
Medium Italic
Bold
Bold Italic
Black
Black Italic

ITC Souvenir®
Light
Light Italic
Medium
Medium Italic
Demi
Demi Italic
Bold
Bold Italic

ITC Symbol®
Book
Book Italic
Medium
Medium Italic
Bold
Bold Italic
Black
Black Italic

ITC Tiffany
Light
Light Italic
Medium
Medium Italic
Demi
Demi Italic
Heavy
Heavy Italic

ITC Usherwood®
Book
Book Italic
Medium
Medium Italic
Bold
Bold Italic
Black
Black Italic

V

ITC Veljovic®
Book
Book Italic
Medium
Medium Italic
Bold
Bold Italic
Black
Black Italic

ITC Weidemann®
Book
Book Italic
Medium
Medium Italic
Bold
Bold Italic
Black
Black Italic

ITC Zapf Book®
Light
Light Italic
Medium
Medium Italic
Demi
Demi Italic
Heavy
Heavy Italic

ITC Zapf Chancery®
Light
Light Italic
Medium
Medium Italic
Demi
Bold

ITC Zapf International®
Light
Light Italic
Medium
Medium Italic
Demi
Demi Italic
Heavy
Heavy Italic

Figure 7.3: Basic characteristics of type

Type categories	General characteristics					
1. Sloping e-Bar (Venetian Serif) Nos 1-34 e.g. **6** Kennerley, **19** Centaur, **30** ITC Souvenir, and **32** Italian Old Style (Monotype).	little contrast	e-bar sloped	angled or vertical stress	oblique ascender serif (not always)	*foot serif often oblique (not always)*	oblique lower case serif (not always)	SLOPING E-BAR (VENETIAN SERIF)
2. Angled Stress/Oblique Serifs (Old Style Serif) Nos 35-53 e.g. **35** Bembo, **39** Plantin, **44** Trump Mediaeval and **53** Times New Roman (Monotype).	medium contrast	e-bar horizontal	angled stress	oblique ascender serif	*oblique foot serif*	oblique lower case serif	ANGLED STRESS OBLIQUE SERIFS (OLD STYLE SERIF)
3. Vertical Stress/Oblique Serifs (Transitional Serif) Nos 54-110 e.g. **61** Caslon 540, **78** Baskerville 169 (Monotype), **92** Garamond (Stempel) and **105** Romulus.	good contrast	e-bar horizontal	stress vertical (or nearly so)	oblique serifs	*foot serif usually level (not always)*	oblique lower case serif	VERTICAL STRESS OBLIQUE SERIFS (TRANSITIONAL SERIF)
4. Vertical Stress/Straight Serifs (New Transitional Serif) e.g. **111** Joanna, **119** Century Schoolbook, **123** Cheltenham, and **138** Melior.	little contrast	e-bar horizontal	vertical stress		*straight serifs (some slightly oblique)*	straight serif in lower case (some oblique)	VERTICAL STRESS STRAIGHT SERIFS (NEW TRANSITIONAL)
5. Abrupt Contrast/Straight Serifs (Modern Serif) Nos 151-187 e.g. **153** Bauer Bodoni, **161** Walbaum (Linotype), **174** Caledonia and **185** Scotch Roman.	abrupt contrast	e-bar horizontal	vertical stress	line or bracketed serifs	straight serifs	straight serifs	ABRUPT CONTRAST STRAIGHT SERIFS (MODERN SERIF)
6. Slab Serif Nos 188-217 e.g. **197** Rockwell, **203** Schadow Antiqua, **209** Clarendon (Linotype), and **214** ITC American Typewriter.	little or no contrast	square slab serifs	single storey / double storey	bracketed serifs	single storey / double storey	rounded serif	SLAB SERIF
7. Wedge Serif (Hybrid Serif) Nos 218-240 e.g. **218** Albertus, **233** Meridien, **236** Copperplate Gothic and **240** Romic.	poor contrast	wedge-ended serifs	wedge-shaped serifs		fine line terminals	half serif only	WEDGE SERIF (HYBRID SERIF)
8. Sans Serif Nos 245-304 e.g. **254** Futura, **259** Gill Sans, **267** Univers 55 and **279** Helvetica.	little or no contrast	wide / medium / narrow (no spur)	wide / medium / narrow (spur)		special shape (rounded)		SANS SERIF

blacker than regular faces, and other faces that are lighter than regular faces.

Italic typefaces An italic face is a slanted face, modeled after handwriting (invented in 1501 by Aldus Manutius). Most typefaces have regular versions and italic ones, which are often used

FIGURE 7.3
Basic characteristics of type.

for emphasis. In scholarly writing, for example, we use italics to indicate the names of books and foreign words and phrases, or to emphasize a word or passage in some text.

Capital letters   The capital (uppercase) is generally larger and higher than the lowercase letter and is used at the beginnings of sentences for titles and display purposes. It is difficult to read long passages of material set in uppercase.

Lowercase letters   These letters have a different design from capital letters and are not just smaller capital letters. Lowercase letters have ascenders and descenders that give variety and facilitate distinguishing between letters.

To see the difference between reading something entirely in capitals and reading something in capitals and lowercase type, look at the following example.

WE THE PEOPLE OF THE UNITED STATES, IN ORDER TO FORM A MORE PERFECT UNION, ESTABLISH JUSTICE, INSURE DOMESTIC TRANQUILITY, PROVIDE FOR THE COMMON DEFENSE, PROMOTE THE GENERAL WELFARE, AND SECURE THE BLESSINGS OF LIBERTY TO OURSELVES AND OUR POSTERITY, DO ORDAIN AND ESTABLISH THIS CONSTITUTION FOR THE UNITED STATES OF AMERICA.

We the People of the United States, in Order to form a more perfect Union, establish Justice, insure domestic Tranquility, provide for the common defense, promote the general Welfare, and secure the Blessings of Liberty to ourselves and our Posterity, do ordain and establish this CONSTITUTION for the United States of America.

It is obvious that the second passage is much easier to read than the first passage. There is more white space around the letters in the second passage, which seems to facilitate comprehension.

Readability is not always a function of the size of the type. We can see that the passage done in capitals has larger type but is more difficult to read. Readability is connected to the way the combination of letters creates a quickly perceived word image.

Points   Type sizes were, at one time, identified by name, but this convention has given way to identifying them by points. (The point system was developed in France in 1737 by Pierre Simon Fournier.) A point is about 1/72 inch. Twelve points are known as a pica. When describing the size of type, we use points and thus might talk about 12-point type or 18-point type. Figure 7.4 shows examples of type size.

BOOK

Excellence in typography is the result of nothing more than an attitude. Its appeal comes from the understanding used in its planning; the designer must care. In contemporary advertising the perfect integration of design elements often demands unorthodox typography. It may require the use of compact spacing, minus leading, unusual sizes and weights; whatever is needed to improve appearance and impact. Stating specific principles or guides on the subject of typography is difficult because the principle applying to one job may not fit the next. No two jobs are identical even if the same point sizes are used. It is worthwhile to emphasize here that in modern typography almost all typ
6 POINT

Excellence in typography is the result of nothing more than an attitude. Its appeal comes from the understanding used in its planning; the designer must care. In contemporary advertising the perfect integration of design elements often demands unorthodox typography. It may require the use of compact spacing, minus leading, unusual sizes and weights; whatever is needed to improve appearance and impact. Stating specific principles or guides on the subject of typography is difficult because the principle applying to one job may not fit the next. No two jobs are identical even if the same po
7 POINT

Excellence in typography is the result of nothing more than an attitude. Its appeal comes from the understanding used in its planning; the designer must care. In contemporary advertising the perfect integration of design elements often demands unorthodox typography. It may require the use of compact spacing, minus leading, unusual sizes and weights; whatever is needed to improve appearance and impact. Stating specific principles or guides on the subject of typography is difficult because the principle applying to one jo
8 POINT

Excellence in typography is the result of nothing more than an attitude. Its appeal comes from the understanding used in its planning; the designer must care. In contemporary advertising the perfect integration of design elements often demands unorthodox typography. It may require the use of compact spacing, minus leading, unusual sizes and weights; whatever is needed to improve appearance and impact. Stating specific principles or guides on the subject of typ
9 POINT

Excellence in typography is the result of nothing more than an attitude. Its appeal comes from the understanding used in its planning; the designer must care. In contemporary advertising the perfect integration of design elements often demands unorthodox typography. It may require the use of compact spacing, minus leading, unusual sizes and weights; whatever is needed to improve appearance and impact. Stating speci
10 POINT

BOLD

Excellence in typography is the result of nothing more than an attitude. Its appeal comes from the understanding used in its planning; the designer must care. In contemporary advertising the perfect integration of design elements often demands unorthodox typography. It may require the use of compact spacing, minus leading, unusual sizes and weights; whatever is needed to improve appearance and impact. Stating specific principles or guides on the subject of typography is difficult because the principle applying to one job may not fit the next. No two jobs are identical even if the same point sizes are used. It is worthwhile to emphasize here th

Excellence in typography is the result of nothing more than an attitude. Its appeal comes from the understanding used in its planning; the designer must care. In contemporary advertising the perfect integration of design elements often demands unorthodox typography. It may require the use of compact spacing, minus leading, unusual sizes and weights; whatever is needed to improve appearance and impact. Stating specific principles or guides on the subject of typography is difficult because the principle applying to one job may not fit the next. No two jobs ar

Excellence in typography is the result of nothing more than an attitude. Its appeal comes from the understanding used in its planning; the designer must care. In contemporary advertising the perfect integration of design elements often demands unorthodox typography. It may require the use of compact spacing, minus leading, unusual sizes and weights; whatever is needed to improve appearance and impact. Stating specific principles or guides on the subject of typography is difficult because the prin

Excellence in typography is the result of nothing more than an attitude. Its appeal comes from the understanding used in its planning; the designer must care. In contemporary advertising the perfect integration of design elements often demands unorthodox typography. It may require the use of compact spacing, minus leading, unusual sizes and weights; whatever is needed to improve appearance and impact. Stating specific principles or guides o

Excellence in typography is the result of nothing more than an attitude. Its appeal comes from the understanding used in its planning; the designer must care. In contemporary advertising the perfect integration of design elements often demands unorthodox typography. It may require the use of compact spacing, minus leading, unusual sizes and weights; whatever is needed to improve appearance and im

FIGURE 7.4
Examples of typeface sizes and font variations within one type family. Not only are there numerous typefaces, but each typeface comes in many styles and different sizes.

BOOK ITALIC

Excellence in typography is the result of nothing more than an attitude. Its appeal comes from the understanding used in its planning; the designer must care. In contemporary advertising the perfect integration of design elements often demands unorthodox typography. It may require the use of compact spacing, minus leading, unusual sizes and weights; whatever is needed to improve appearance and impact. Stating specific principles or guides on the subject of typography is difficult because the principle applying to one job may not fit the next. No two jobs are identical even if the same point sizes are used. It is worthwhile to emphasize here that in modern typography almost all typefaces, old or new, are utilized. Modern typography appeal co
6 POINT

Excellence in typography is the result of nothing more than an attitude. Its appeal comes from the understanding used in its planning; the designer must care. In contemporary advertising the perfect integration of design elements often demands unorthodox typography. It may require the use of compact spacing, minus leading, unusual sizes and weights; whatever is needed to improve appearance and impact. Stating specific principles or guides on the subject of typography is difficult because the principle applying to one job may not fit the next. No two jobs are identical even if the same point sizes are used. It is worthwhile to emphasize here t
7 POINT

Excellence in typography is the result of nothing more than an attitude. Its appeal comes from the understanding used in its planning; the designer must care. In contemporary advertising the perfect integration of design elements often demands unorthodox typography. It may require the use of compact spacing, minus leading, unusual sizes and weights; whatever is needed to improve appearance and impact. Stating specific principles or guides on the subject of typography is difficult because the principle applying to one job may not fit the next. No two jobs are identi
8 POINT

Excellence in typography is the result of nothing more than an attitude. Its appeal comes from the understanding used in its planning; the designer must care. In contemporary advertising the perfect integration of design elements often demands unorthodox typography. It may require the use of compact spacing, minus leading, unusual sizes and weights; whatever is needed to improve appearance and impact. Stating specific principles or guides on the subject of typography is difficult because the principle
9 POINT

Excellence in typography is the result of nothing more than an attitude. Its appeal comes from the understanding used in its planning; the designer must care. In contemporary advertising the perfect integration of design elements often demands unorthodox typography. It may require the use of compact spacing, minus leading, unusual sizes and weights; whatever is needed to improve appearance and impact. Stating specific principles or guides on the subject
10 POINT

BOLD ITALIC

Excellence in typography is the result of nothing more than an attitude. Its appeal comes from the understanding used in its planning; the designer must care. In contemporary advertising the perfect integration of design elements often demands unorthodox typography. It may require the use of compact spacing, minus leading, unusual sizes and weights; whatever is needed to improve appearance and impact. Stating specific principles or guides on the subject of typography is difficult because the principle applying to one job may not fit the next. No two jobs are identical even if the same point sizes are used. It is worthwhile to emphasize here that in modern typography almost

Excellence in typography is the result of nothing more than an attitude. Its appeal comes from the understanding used in its planning; the designer must care. In contemporary advertising the perfect integration of design elements often demands unorthodox typography. It may require the use of compact spacing, minus leading, unusual sizes and weights; whatever is needed to improve appearance and impact. Stating specific principles or guides on the subject of typography is difficult because the principle applying to one job may not fit the next. No two jobs are identical even if the same po

Excellence in typography is the result of nothing more than an attitude. Its appeal comes from the understanding used in its planning; the designer must care. In contemporary advertising the perfect integration of design elements often demands unorthodox typography. It may require the use of compact spacing, minus leading, unusual sizes and weights; whatever is needed to improve appearance and impact. Stating specific principles or guides on the subject of typography is difficult because the principle applying to one job may

Excellence in typography is the result of nothing more than an attitude. Its appeal comes from the understanding used in its planning; the designer must care. In contemporary advertising the perfect integration of design elements often demands unorthodox typography. It may require the use of compact spacing, minus leading, unusual sizes and weights; whatever is needed to improve appearance and impact. Stating specific principles or guides on the subject of typograp

Excellence in typography is the result of nothing more than an attitude. Its appeal comes from the understanding used in its planning; the designer must care. In contemporary advertising the perfect integration of design elements often demands unorthodox typography. It may require the use of compact spacing, minus leading, unusual sizes and weights; whatever is needed to improve appearance and impact. Stating specific p

Condensed and Expanded Typefaces Some typefaces have very narrow letters and are known as condensed faces. These faces allow one to print more text in a given area than if one uses regular faces. There are also expanded faces, which feature very wide letters and use more space than regular faces and much more space than condensed faces.

It is obvious from this brief introduction to typography that typefaces play an important role in transmitting information and that the way a message is presented has a great deal of significance. Typography is a highly skilled art and plays an important role in shaping the way people respond to printed matter. Typographers often say that typography should be "invisible" and should not be noticed by the reader; that is, it should not call attention to itself since the purpose of printing is to produce material that is read. In such cases, it is all the more powerful.

Maximizing the Impact of Type

Let's list some of the considerations to be kept in mind when laying out a print advertisement, a newsletter, or anything that has a visual dimension to it.

Typeface We have already seen that the choice of typefaces is important, since different typefaces have distinctive personalities. Each typeface is a means of managing impressions in the minds of readers. And the typeface must be coordinated with any drawings or photographs being used in the visual field. In the case of advertisements or other kinds of promotional literature, for example, the typefaces must fit with the "image" of the product that is to be created or reinforced (Figure 7.5).

Size of the face We are also affected by the size of a given typeface, since size affects the way we respond to the design of individual letters.

Leading The amount of white space between the lines of print is referred to as *leading*. We respond, unconsciously, to extremely minute changes in the amount of leading, since the leading can give printed material a light and open look or, conversely, a heavy, dense look (Figure 7.6).

Spacing between letters Here, too, small differences have major consequences. This holds true especially in the display aspects of printing, where the letters are relatively large and the eye can see when letters are too close to one another, or the reverse. Experts pay great attention to these things; although they may seem trivial, if you think of an advertisement, newsletter, brochure, or the design of a magazine or other publication as a means of

FIGURE 7.5
Here we see examples of the impact of different typefaces and type sizes on a visual image.

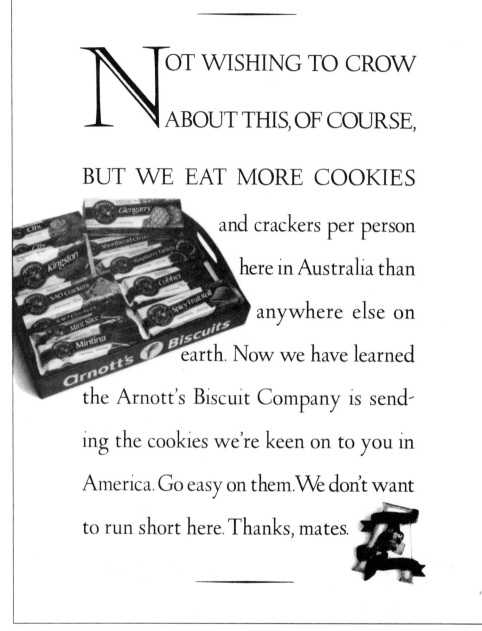

NOT WISHING TO CROW ABOUT THIS, OF COURSE, BUT WE EAT MORE COOKIES and crackers per person here in Australia than anywhere else on earth. Now we have learned the Arnott's Biscuit Company is sending the cookies we're keen on to you in America. Go easy on them. We don't want to run short here. Thanks, mates.

FIGURE 7.6

Arnott's Biscuits advertisement. Note the amount of leading in this advertisement and the effect this has on the image. This advertisement was hand-set to give it a different and more refined look than most printed matter, which is photoset.

shaping people's perceptions, small things add up to big differences in effectiveness and impact.

Margins In recent years, the notion of having ragged right margins (that is, margins that do not line up) has become popular. The ragged right margin conveys a different feeling than a flush right (or justified), margin does — it has a less formal and, some would say, more contemporary feel to it. The size of top and bottom margins and how the text is placed relative to photographs, drawings, or other graphic material also affects the final image.

Design This term is used to cover the whole matter of how the different elements in a visual field are placed in relation to one another. Artists and designers have different sensibilities (and in the case of advertising, so do clients, who sometimes affect the outcome), which is why a group of six art directors would each turn out different-looking advertisements, even if given the same elements to work with: a photograph and text set into type.

General Principles of Design

The material we've discussed so far has applied to visual fields in general and to specific kinds of visual materials — advertisements, brochures, manuals, magazines, etc. The specific topics we've mentioned can be subsumed under some more general principles of design, many of which have been discussed or alluded to earlier places in this book. They are brought together here.

Balance

This term refers to the way basic elements in a design relate to one another. We've already discussed axial or formal balance and its opposite, dynamic or informal balance. Each generates a different kind of response. In general, we must put the elements in a design into some kind of relationship that is visually effective and that accomplishes the mission of the work. Elements have different weights, depending upon such things as size, shape, and color; and these weights must be tied together in some way to generate a kind of balance that is visually functional.

Proportion

Here we are dealing with the size of different elements in a design. Recall from Chapter 2 that if balance involves the way elements relate to one another around imaginary vertical and horizontal axes, proportion involves how they relate to one another in general, relative to the size or area of the visual field being utilized—that is, the size of the advertisement, brochure, magazine or whatever (Figure 7.7).

Let us take the example of a magazine cover. The size of the title is of some consequence. If it is too large and the typeface is too heavy (that is, out of proportion), the cover seems top-heavy and is disturbing. We all have a sense of correct proportions; when visual phenomena violate these notions or codes, we are bothered. Sometimes, of course, codes are violated on purpose, to achieve a particular effect. Tastes always are changing when it comes to design, and what seems beautiful and tasteful and exciting one year can seem dull and banal a few years later.

Movement

Here we are talking about the way elements in a composition lead our eyes along and force them to scan the composition for information. This movement (described by Zettl as involving what he calls "vectors") is accomplished by various means, such as line and shape and color. We know that the eye tends to favor the upper left corner in any visual field; it can then be drawn to various parts of the field by shapes and lines and other design elements.

Even when we look at a sculpture or a simple design, the eye scans in interesting ways. We tend to trace over the outline of a visual and follow lines and shapes that are presented to us by artists and designers. The fact that we seek movement and that visual phenomena can generate visual excitement and more or less "force" our eyes to move in certain directions is of considerable use to people in advertising, but is used by all visual artists.

Contrast

Earlier it was suggested that concepts have no meaning in themselves but only in relation to other concepts—with opposition being the most important relationship. The same applies to visual phenomena. It is through contrasts, difference in size, shape, color, etc., that elements in a visual field have the meaning they have. We know, for example, that a square of red looks

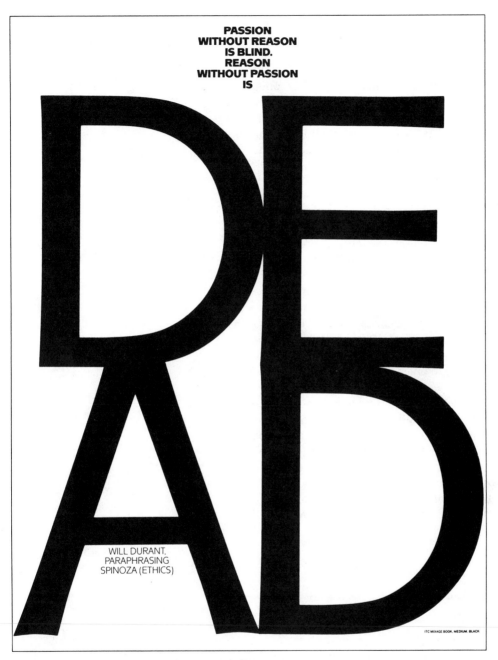

PASSION
WITHOUT REASON
IS BLIND.
REASON
WITHOUT PASSION
IS

DEAD

WILL DURANT,
PARAPHRASING
SPINOZA (ETHICS)

ITC MIXAGE BOOK, MEDIUM, BLACK

FIGURE 7.7

"Thoughts" page from *U&lc*. The letters forming the word "DEAD" are very large in proportion to the rest of the message. This design works because the letters become a design element with a powerful aesthetic appeal. This example shows that in graphic design all kinds of possibilities exist and the laws of proportion, which this page violates, are extremely flexible.

General Principles of Design | 143

different with a gray background than with an orange background. The figure is affected by the ground.

In some cases, where we wish elements to stand out, we emphasize contrast and thus have something simple standing against or placed in opposition to something busy, or something dark against something light. Contrasts generate attention. The power of color contrasts was used by Pop artists and Op artists to generate certain effects. Very strong colors and bright color contrasts also have certain class implications or associations and thus must be used with care.

Unity

This term refers to the way all the elements in a composition or visual field relate to one another and produce a sense of completeness and wholeness. Related to unity is a Gestalt effect, a psychological and aesthetic response that is greater than the sum of its parts. In other words, the entire image may produce a response that is greater than would be produced by adding the various elements in the visual field (Figure 7.8). The opposite of unity is fragmentation, which suggests that the elements in the composition don't relate to one another, producing a sense that the work is incomplete.

In some cases, artists don't wish to generate a unified effect and so purposely use fragmentation to achieve a particular effect that they desire. *There are no rules in design and composition that are absolute, and the best designers and artists often violate rules.* In thinking about design, one should consider the effect desired first and then work to achieve that effect, using whatever techniques one can to achieve it. So we work backwards, from the desired effect to whatever can be done to generate that effect.

Design Examples

Two Versions of a Page

To show how changes in typography and design can give a publication a different look, consider Figures 7.9 and 7.10. It shows two "pages" that use the same copy but are worlds apart in terms of the way they look.

FIGURE 7.8
Front pages of selected newspapers. Look at the *Wall Street Journal* issue of February 16, 1988 (page 145). This is an excellent example of typographic unity. The headlines, subheads, and textual matter are all relatively similar in size, and the illustrations are all small. This page projects an image of sobriety and high seriousness. Contrast this with the front pages from the *San Francisco Examiner* issue of March 13, 1988 (page 146), and the issue of *USA Today* of October 22, 1987 (page 147). The latter two papers have much different personalities, which are reflected on their front pages.

BUSINESS

COLLEGE TUITION

CELLULAR TELEPHONES

San Francisco Examiner

$1.00 | SUNDAY, MARCH 13, 1988 | ★ ★ ★ ★ LATE EDITION

AIDS, S.F. addicts: There's hope

First of two parts

By Jayne Garrison
OF THE EXAMINER STAFF

The second wave of AIDS sweeping through East Coast drug addicts has yet to hit the shores of the Pacific with the same ferocity, and researchers say evidence is growing that it need never hit.

"It's perfectly controllable," says UC-San Francisco epidemiologist Andrew Moss. "My position is, you can deal with this stuff.... The best solution is to find them (addicts) and treat them."

The devastating march of the human immunodeficiency virus (HIV), the virus that causes AIDS, through homosexual communities followed nearly identical patterns in New York City and San Francisco, infecting half the gay men in both cities. Officials feared it was only a matter of time before the tidal wave of HIV overwhelmed addicts in San Francisco, as it has in New York.

But it hasn't.

Seven years into the AIDS epidemic, heterosexual drug users account for just 3 percent of cases statewide and 1.4 percent of the cases in San Francisco, compared with 31 percent in New York City. (Drug users who are gay or bisexual account for 12 percent of San Francisco cases.)

About 15 percent of The City's 13,000 heterosexual heroin and speed addicts are believed infected with HIV but are not yet sick. This compares with an estimated 60 percent of the addicts in New York.

Although the San Francisco numbers are low compared with East Coast cities, they are grim enough. In Los Angeles, officials say, less than 3 percent of its addicts are infected. In Alameda County, the most recent study of 200 addicts at methadone clinics showed 3 percent were infected.

Moreover, the rate of new infection among drug users in San Francisco is rising steadily at 3 percent annually — roughly 300 people a year. Yet even with these causes for concern, researchers say the enormous wave of AIDS that

— See AIDS, A-9

Proposition 69 losing

A new Examiner/NewsCenter 4 poll shows that California voters oppose a Lyndon Larouche-backed AIDS initiative on the June ballot by 60 percent to 32 percent.

Page A-8

Associated Press

Anti-Noriega demonstrators take to the streets in Panama

Passive majority living amid crisis in Panama

By Raul Ramirez
OF THE EXAMINER STAFF

PANAMA CITY, Panama — Peter Downing keeps a plastic water bottle and a handkerchief in his knapsack to ease the sting of tear gas. Stephen and Joyce Knupt have relearned the joy of home cooking. And, for now, Harold H. Brown is forgoing the company of his favorite bar hostess.

That's how some of the nearly 50,000 U.S. citizens who live in Panama are adjusting to the deepening political crisis that has made tear gas, burning barricades and anti-American slogans daily fare in this capital city by the canal.

Despite the vitriolic showdown between the U.S. government and Panama's military ruler, Gen. Manuel Antonio Noriega, Americans here — from military men to life-long canal workers — say they do not fear for their personal safety.

"Panamanians are too accus-

— See PANAMA, A-11

Chip shortage threatens U.S. computer firms

By Paul Freiberger
OF THE EXAMINER STAFF

A shortage of Japanese computer chips is causing a crisis in Silicon Valley and throughout the computer industry.

As a result, the price of personal computers and related products is starting to rise. Some experts foresee a major slump if the trend continues, with consequent loss of jobs, shake-out of companies, transfer of firms overseas and stalling of innovation. The crisis may also help Japanese companies improve their position in computer-related markets, some observers fear.

"Supply is going from bad to worse," said Clint Cowan, product manager with Quadram Corp., a maker of PC add-on products.

The price of some Japanese memory chips has more than doubled in the past year. Chips that sold for $2.15 a year ago now are in short supply and cost $2.80 to $5 when bought under contract. To obtain extra supplies, companies often must buy chips on the spot market at a higher price.

Some U.S. computer executives are exasperated to the point of discussing moving their manufacturing facilities out of the country.

"The price of chips is out of hand," said Jim Cavuto, editor of Micro Publishing Report, an industry newsletter. "Chips are the fuel of the computer industry. It

— See CHIPS, back page

Reuter

Israelis rally for peace

Thousands of Israeli "Peace Now" demonstrators flood Tel Aviv to urge Prime Minister Yitzhak Shamir to support a U.S.-sponsored peace initiative. Story/Page A-12

Anatomy of a drug dealer's murder

Boyhood pals are prime suspects in 2-year-old slaying

By Lance Williams
OF THE EXAMINER STAFF

Like the men suspected of his murder, Brian Murray, 31, was a big-league drug dealer from St. Francis Wood — a son of the middle class who put all his charm, brains and ambition into a lucrative career selling cocaine in $100,000 lots.

He disappeared in November 1986 — apparently en route to a meeting regarding a $250,000 cocaine score. His body was found a month later in San Francisco Bay, bound and hung with body-builder's weights.

Last week, San Francisco police cracked the 2-year-old mystery of Murray's murder, naming two men they say killed the drug dealer and dumped his body after robbing him of $70,000.

They arrested 29-year-old Dan Mugnolo, a convicted drug dealer and self-described cocaine addict, in his cell at the Marin County jail. He was charged with murder and is being held without bail.

A second suspect named in an affidavit is David Henry, 36, a boyhood friend of the victim who is serving a 13-year sentence at Terminal Island for selling $850,000 in cocaine to an undercover agent.

To investigators, the remarkable thing about Murray's alleged killers is that they are so much like their victim — young men from one of The City's finest neighborhoods who played together in the neighborhood park, attended parochial schools and, as adults, became so absorbed in the cocaine trade that it dominated their lives.

"They all grew up in St. Francis Wood or a stone's throw away, and they all turned out to be drug dealers," says Inspector Edward Erdelatz, who with his partner Jeffrey Brosch investigated the case.

According to people who knew him, Murray was a handsome, witty Irish-Catholic who with his four brothers and one sister grew up in the big family home on Santa Clara Avenue.

His father, now dead, was a middle-level executive who managed to afford a home in that exclusive neighborhood only through considerable sacrifice. The brothers recall that while growing up they were

— See BRIAN, back page

Jackson wins S.C.

Democratic presidential candidate Jesse Jackson won the Democratic precinct caucuses Saturday in his native South Carolina. Page A-8

Bush may regret clinching party nomination so early

By John Jacobs
EXAMINER CHIEF POLITICAL WRITER

ANALYSIS

CHICAGO — Vice President Bush, on the verge of winning the GOP presidential nomination, faces potentially great advantages but also major dangers.

While his chief rival, Sen. Bob Dole of Kansas, dithered and sent mixed signals about whether his campaign would even continue here last week, Bush seemed poised for another substantial victory in the Illinois primary Tuesday.

That could change by voting day. But a Bush victory and a subsequent Dole withdrawal would wrap up the nomination earlier than any non-inc[illegible] GOP candidate in recent m[illegible].

While saving money and resources, Bush runs the risk of losing the spotlight until the August convention, unless he gets hit with negative publicity from the Iran-contra scandal, some experts said.

Dole is at least partly to blame for his predicament. His fumblings last week weren't the first of his organization's problems. He stepped all over himself Thursday by canceling most of his Illinois TV advertising to "rethink" his strategy. That came amid reports that top aides had advised him to drop out even before Tuesday's voting.

He now insists he's in the race to

— See GOP, A-10

INSIDE

Editor's Report
Super break: William Randolph Hearst Jr. says it's time for a political break now that Super Tuesday is over. Page A-19

National
Midwest paralyzed: A major snowstorm shuts down travel in the upper Midwest. Page A-5

Foreign
Religion with gusto: With the fastest-growing church in the world in Seoul, Koreans live their religion with gusto. Page A-12
Cocaine connection: Haiti now finds itself in the spotlight as a key link in the Caribbean drugs-and-arms trade. Page A-13

Metro
Morgan Hill booming: A onetime wide spot in the road, Morgan Hill has quietly become the fastest-growing town in booming Santa Clara County. Page B-1

Sports
Stanford's glory days: Spring of '42 was the last time Stanford's basketball team played in a postseason tournament. Page C-1

Opera director: Lotfi Mansouri, the San Francisco Opera's new general director, talks with Examiner critic Allan Ulrich. Page A-3

Style
VCR libraries: Where once their shelves were filled with books, VCR aficionados now are building cassette libraries. Page E-1

Real Estate
'Ticky Tacky' Daly City: The city is no longer just a place of "ticky tacky" boxes as a 1960s song said. Page F-1

Travel
Destination Europe: From a stagecoach tour of southern Germany to super skiing on the Swiss slopes. Page T-1

Image
Oakland's troubles: Former Examiner Writer In Residence Ishmael Reed offers a citizens lament on Oakland's waring drug gangs. The magazine

Summary of the news/Page A-2

Robert Bruss	F-6	Obituaries	B-7
Business	D-1	Outdoors	C-14
Editorials	A-18	Real Estate	F-1
Ann Landers	E-2	Scoreboard	C-12
Bill Mandel	B-3	Sports	C-1
Rob Morse	A-2	Style	E-1
Cyra McF'n	E-1	Weather	B-2

Vol. 1988, No. 11

Not enough Bay homes for buyers

By Corrie M. Anders
OF THE EXAMINER STAFF

The worst shortage of homes for sale in a decade is leaving Bay Area buyers frustrated and chagrined as the spring home-buying season gets under way.

From Pleasanton to Novato to San Francisco, buyers are grabbing what homes there are as soon as they become available — sometimes offering more money than the asking price. Some buyers are settling for less than what they want in order to buy now.

Developers of single-family subdivisions have long waiting lists of buyers after showing prospects little more than floor plans and a dream. One Redwood Shores developer on the Peninsula has more than 750 buyers for 134 homes that won't start hitting the market until next month.

"There are just buyers galore," said Martha "Dolly" Toms, senior vice president for Grubb & Ellis Co. "An open house will have 50 people going through, and it's terribly frustrating because they can't buy anything."

Spring typically is the busiest time of the year for home buyers, and house hunting in the Bay Area — one of the most expensive markets in the country — is never easy.

But this year the problem is exacerbated by a supply-and-demand ratio way out of kilter. In addition to a lack of desirable homes on the market, demand has jumped sharply, fueled by mortgage interest rates below 10 percent, a fear of rising home prices and the realization by some that the 1986 tax re-

— See HOMES, back page

an important role in transmitting information and that the way a message is presented has a great deal of significance. Typography is a highly skilled art and plays an important role in shaping the way people respond to printed matter. Typographers often say that typography should be "invisible" and should not be noticed by the reader.

DESIGNING THE VISUAL FIELD

Let me list some of the considerations to be kept in mind when laying out a print advertisement, a newsletter, or anything that has a visual dimension.

A. The Typeface

It has already been suggested that the choice of typefaces is important, since different typefaces have distinctive personalities. Each typeface is a means of managing impressions in the minds of readers. And the typeface must be coordinated with any drawings or photographs being used in the visual field. In the case of advertisements, for example, the typefaces must fit with the "image" of the product that is to be created or reinforced.

> *Artists and designers have different sensibilities (and in the case of advertising, so do clients) who sometimes affect things, which is why a group of six art directors would each turn out different looking advertisements, even if given the same elements to work with.[1]*

B. The Size of the Face

We are also affected by the size of a given typeface, since size affects the way we respond. to the design of individual letters.

The material discussed to this point was applied to visual fields in general and to specific kinds of visual materials – advertisements, brochures, manual, magazines, etc. The topics mentioned can be subsumed under some more general principles of design, many of which have been mentioned or alluded to in various places in this book. They

[1] Op cit. Berger, p. 128.

FIGURE 7.9
Here is a poorly designed page. What's wrong with it? Why doesn't it work?

an important role in transmitting information and that the way a message is presented has a great deal of significance. Typography is a highly skilled art and plays an important role in shaping the way people respond to printed matter. Typographers often say that typography should be "invisible" and should not be noticed by the reader.

DESIGNING THE VISUAL FIELD

Let me list some of the considerations to be kept in mind when laying out a print advertisement, a newsletter, or anything that has a visual dimension.

A. The Typeface It has already been suggested that the choice of type-faces is important, since different typeface have distinctive personalities. Each typeface is a means of managing impression in the minds of readers. And the typeface must be coordinated with any drawings or photographs being used in the visual field. In the case of advertisements, for example, the typefaces must fit with the "image" of the product that is to be created or reinforced.

> *Artists and designers have different sensibilities (and in the case of advertising, so do clients) who sometimes affect things, which is why a group of six art directors would each turn out different looking advertisements, even if given the same elements to work with.*[1]

B. The Size of the Face We are also affected by the size of a given typeface, since size affects the way we respond. to the design of individual letters.

The material discussed to this point was applied to visual fields in general and to specific kinds of visual materials – advertisements, brochures, manual, magazines, etc. The topics mentioned can be subsumed under some more general principles of design, many of which have been mentioned or alluded to in various places in this book. They are discussed below.

[1] Op cit. Berger, p. 123.

FIGURE 7.10
Here is a well-designed page that contains the same material as the page in Figure 7.9 but is set using different typefaces and a different layout. What is it about the good design that makes it pleasing to the eye and effective?

Examine the typography and design in Figure 7.9 and Figure 7.10 in terms of the following considerations, which differentiate the two pages:

1. The right margins for the text. One is flush right and the other is ragged right. What difference does this make?
2. The use of headline faces and display faces. If they are too strong, the page seems top-heavy; if they are too weak, you don't get adequate display and emphasis.
3. The weight of the italics and their visibility.
4. The size of the side margins and where the text is placed on the page relative to the margins.
5. The margins on the top and bottom of the page.
6. The lightness or heaviness of the text face.
7. The size of the text face.
8. The spacing between lines in the text face.

The Talmud

The Talmud is a compendium of the oral law of the Jews, gathered together many hundreds of years ago and subject to the scrutiny and analysis of numerous rabbis and scholars for an extended period of time. The typography of the Talmud is very interesting because different typefaces were used to represent the ideas of the most important commentators. On a given page of the Talmud one might find four or five typefaces, snaking up and down the page, each reflecting an opinion on the main topic of the page, always printed in the largest and heaviest typeface. A typical page from the Talmud is shown in Figure 7.11.

The main section is in heavy type and looks like an inverted T. Then, above it and below it, in different typefaces, are commentaries by some of its classic interpreters. The Talmud runs to many, many volumes and is a work of extraordinary complexity and intellectual sophistication, full of astounding feats of logical deduction and brilliant insights into the human condition. It is impossible to give more than a brief sense of what it is like or of the incredible number of interpretations of ideas and events found in it.

This use of different typefaces to suggest different views is not limited to the Talmud. The page from a business magazine that is shown in Figure 7.12 also employs different faces to suggest different ideas and points of view. Note also, on this page, the exaggerated size of the quote marks and how the typographer uses ragged right for the body type and ragged left for the quoted material in the margins.

Many of the elements we discussed earlier in the book such as the use of white space, formal and informal balance, and contrast go into the design of a book, magazine, or advertisement. There are also the aesthetic sensibilities of the audience to consider: certain designs that may appeal to "upscale" people will not appeal to "downscale" people—and the artists, designers, or creative directors must always make certain that what they do will be appropriate for their audience.

Design and Control

The pages we have just examined reflect something that we seldom think about—namely that design has, in a sense, the power to control people and to evoke certain desired responses. The size of print, the style of print, the heaviness or lightness of print, the size of margins, the arrangement of the block of type on the page—these and countless other seemingly minor matters have a profound impact on how we respond to printed matter and visual phenomena in general (Figure 7.13). When we are browsing through a magazine, do we just glance at an ad and then turn the page, or do we pause for a moment to examine the ad? And if we do pause, what do we look at first? What do we read first?

These matters are of great concern to advertisers, who spend enormous amounts of money on their campaigns. It may be true that you can't tell a book by its cover, but experience tells us you can *sell* a book by its cover.

Supergraphics

Supergraphics reflect an interesting phenomena: that a change in scale leads to a change in identity. Just as comic strip frames became works of art when they were blown up, painted in oils, put into a frame, and purchased by museums and art collectors, so does a word—that is, a group of letters—become an art object, so to speak, when it is enlarged into a supergraphic. The aesthetic components of each letter, which tend to be neglected when the letter is seen normal size, suddenly become visible.

In addition, the spaces and shapes created by huge letters are visually interesting and exciting. With supergraphics, then, we move from the printed page, where the mass of letters has an impact, to the gigantic wall, where a few letters or words and images, blown up to a great size, have an impact.

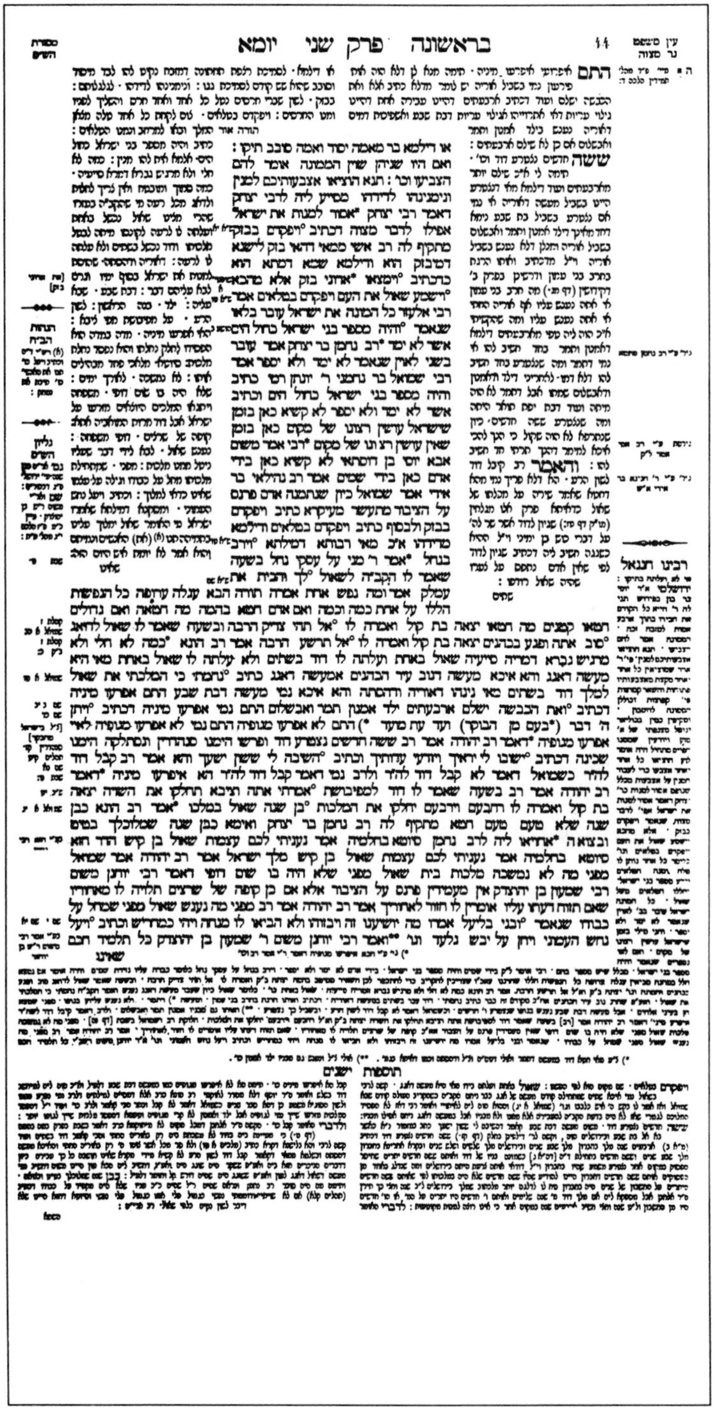

FIGURE 7.11
Page from the Talmud, showing different typefaces that are identified with different commentators. This shows the power of a typeface to confer an identity on someone or some institution.

FIGURE 7.12 (on page 153)
Page from *New Management.* Notice the similarity of this page and the Talmud in terms of use of different typefaces, representing different ideas on a single page.

changes its management system, we will see more powerful American competitors. 99

Akio Morita, Chairman of Sony, put the problem most succinctly:

66 The problem in the United States is management. Instead of meeting the challenge of a changing world, American business today is making small, short-term adjustments by cutting costs, by turning to the government for temporary relief.Success in trade is the result of patience and meticulous preparations with a long period of marketing preparation before the rewards are available. 99

The key to the future lies in how our businesses are managed. Much is being studied, written, and discussed about the changes that are necessary, but too little attention is paid to the personal qualities of managerial leadership and to the dimensions missing in many of today's managers.

Missing Dimensions

While I believe in the usefulness of management science and management systems, of long-range and strategic planning, the challenges we face will not be solved by more and better systems and techniques. While there is need to continue to push the frontiers of knowledge and enhance the contributions of management science, we must not forget that much of management is still art. Effective management is a combination of knowledge and intuition, of position and personality, of environmental constraints and human will, of time and chance.

There is no single theory of management sufficient in scope to guide intelligent action; nonetheless, there are rich conceptual resources that can guide the work of management. We can identify, for example, the qualities that distinguish excellence from mediocrity in managers. The critical dimensions lie, in my judgment, in the ability to orchestrate human talent and to bring the qualitative as well as the quantitative to bear effectively on the solution of complex problems. **David Lilienthal,** founder of the Tennessee Valley Administration and former chairman of the Atomic Energy Commission, expressed the idea this way:

66 The art of management is a high form of leadership, for it seeks to combine the act—the getting something done—with the meaning behind the act. 99

What makes management an artistic activity? For one, effective managers are required to integrate different and conflicting theories and themes. For another, effective managers must be able to engage issues on the level of both fact and feeling, to address questions that lie in the area of overlap between science and philosophy—between the tangible and the intangible. And finally, effective managers must overcome a lack of adequate theory to assist them in integrating talent, task, values, and technology.

Viewing management as an art form does not imply any lack of regard for scientific knowledge. One cannot ignore the impressive base of scholarship in management, in decision theory, in organizational theory. But today there are too few philosophers and too many managerial mechanics—enraptured with technique, never asking questions of meaning and purpose—captives to the bottom line of quarterly earnings without a vision or set of values to guide them. There are too few statesmen. There are too many technicians clothed in power and status, but lacking in heart, mind, and spirit.

How we identify, train, and nourish individuals with the qualities for managerial leadership is the challenge faced by management practitioners and scholars. Given such leaders, our ability to address our economic future is secure. The stakes are large, and the effort imperative.

Increasingly, we must come to face the challenges confronting us with the forthrightness, intelligence, creativity and pragmatism which historically have been the hallmarks of our private enterprise system. I believe that we are beginning to engage in the kind of critical self-appraisal and analysis that can ultimately provide the necessary foundations for New Management and, ultimately, for a national renaissance. I am pleased that this new publication is dedicated to helping managers undertake these crucial changes. For if we continue this process, America can emerge from this period—reinforced and reinvigorated by the experience—with our economy, our society, and our values intact for generations to come.

"Absence of adequate tax incentives for capital investment, obsolete plant and equipment, insufficient research and development, the decline of the work ethic, poor labor relations, and problems with government all contribute to the problem. But in my judgment, management inadequacy is by far the greatest single cause."

"Much is being studied, written, and discussed about the changes that are necessary, but too little attention is paid to the personal qualities of managerial leadership and to the dimensions missing in many of today's managers."

Communiqué

January 1987

Center makes west coast debut

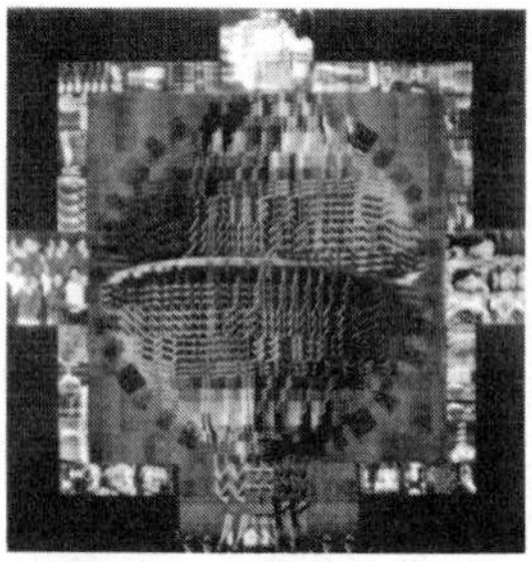

For one day this month the Gannett Center will "move" to California.

On Jan. 26 the Center will present a special public panel discussion titled "Iran and Watergate: For the Media, the Lessons Learned" at the Mark Hopkins Hotel in San Fransisco.

The event, the Center's inaugural program on the west coast, will be held in conjunction with a meeting of the Center's National Advisory Committee and will bring together many of the west's most prominent media professionals and scholars.

National Advisory Committee Chairman Frank H.T. Rhodes and Gannett Center Executive Director Everette Dennis will introduce the Center and its programs, then present the panelists.

Among them will be at least three members of the National Advisory Committee—former *New York Times* reporter Nancy Hicks Maynard, ABC's Ann Compton, and former *Boston Globe* editor Tom Winship. Gannett Center Senior Fellow Burton Benjamin will also be on the panel, and Oakland *Tribune* publisher Bob Maynard and NAC member Michael Sovern, Columbia's president, are tentatively scheduled to participate on the panel also.

Several west coast Associates of the Gannett Center will also attend the program. The Center's Associates Program brings together leaders of many American institutions who bring their special experience and insights to the Center's programs.

Media Message People, the new Gannett Center poster, is free upon request. See p.6.

New fellows bring complementary interests

Five new fellows begin work at the Center in January, examining different aspects of important and interrelated issues, among them the professionalization of journalists and the economic changes affecting newspapers.

The new arrivals are: Ellis Cose, from the University of California at Berkeley; Jeff Greenfield of ABC News; Lawrence McGill of Northwestern University; John Merrill, from Louisiana State University; and Susan Tifft of *Time* magazine.

All five will be in residence at the Center through the spring.

Jeff Greenfield, whose appointment as a fellow was announced in November, will be studying "Media Handling of Unanticipated Domestic Political Crises."

New Senior Fellow John Merrill will be spending a good portion of his time in New York at the United Nations, studying the key people who cover the U.N. for foreign papers and the role of their coverage in forming international

diplomatic opinion. While many studies have looked at the role of American journalists in this process, foreign journalists have been largely ignored.

Ellis Cose's study will also examine a select group of journalists—future ones. "There are interesting leadership changes going on," Cose says, "a changing of the guard in the editorial and business sense. Newspaper companies in the future will be substantially different, and my project is an inquiry into where present and future leaders are trying to take us and their companies."

Looking at the changes in the newspaper business from a different angle, Susan Tifft's project examines "The Coming of a New Economic Order to Media Ownership," a project she developed at least in part by looking at the old economic order: family ownership.

While at the Center, Tifft will also be working on a biography of the Bingham family, the former owners of the Louisville *Courier-Journal.*

Like Cose, new Research Fellow Larry McGill will be examining the way journalists come to positions of leadership, but McGill will focus on the role that particular news beats play in determining whether they get there.

"I once heard someone say that 85 percent of editors come from the political beat," McGill said, "and, as a sociologist, when I hear a precise number like that it sets off bells: Is it true? What values do top news people bring to their jobs? Where do they get them and how do they implement them?"

The new fellows join six others who are continuing fellowships at the Center— Burton Benjamin, Jerrold Footlick, Dan Schiller, Susan Shapiro, Sally Bedell Smith and Michael Moss—and come just as four others have returned to their professional and academic posts. David Anderson has returned to the University of Texas, Herbert Gans and Eleanor Singer have resumed their duties at Columbia, and Chris Ogan is back at Indiana University.

A Gannett Foundation Program at Columbia University

FIGURE 7.13

Communiqué. The newsletter is a very powerful means of communication; it is flexible, inexpensive, and easy to produce.

Conclusions

Some scholars believe that there are certain social, psychological, and political imperatives that flow from the development of movable type and printing. Printing, they suggest, leads to the development of a linear mode of thinking (generated by the lines of type we become used to reading) and, indirectly, to individualism and nationalism.

We need not go into such ramifications here; this brief investigation of a very complicated topic is meant to alert you to the power of type and typography, which in combination with the photographic image (in its various manifestations) and the drawn or painted image so dominates our media and our visual experience.

Applications

1. Duplicate four pages of text from various books and explain how the different typefaces used in them generate different feelings. Consider such matters as: size, leading, weight, margin size, kind of margin (justified right or ragged right), and so on. Use this book as one of the four.

2. Write a short historical essay on the evolution of a typeface that you like.

3. Find an example of typography that you think is particularly bad. Explain why it is bad.

4. Find an example of typography that you think is particularly good. Explain why it is good.

5. Assume a millionaire gave you a great deal of money and told you to create a new magazine. Decide what you would like to do. Choose a title. Then lay out the cover for the first issue. Using printed matter from other magazines, whose style you like, dummy in a few pages, to give a sense of the "look" of the magazine.

6. Find a visual that you like and analyze it according to the principles of design described in this chapter: balance, proportion, movement, contrast, and unity. Do the same thing with a visual that you don't like (which doesn't "work") and explain why.

7. Take photographs of any supergraphics in your living area and analyze them using the criteria described in this chapter.

If you were asked to design supergraphics for the same space, what would you have done differently?

8. What do you think of the notion that the linearity of print has affected society? Will electronic media change things?

Computers and Graphics: Wonders from the Image-Maker

Chapter 8

The Nature of the Computer

Many people have the wrong idea about computers. Computers are electronic machines that can perform manipulations and calculations at incredible speeds, with data, using a program or stored set of instructions. Nevertheless, though computers are capable of incredibly fast operations with numbers, it is better to think of computers as devices that manipulate symbols or visual data rather than as adding machines or calculators. The most important symbol the computer can manipulate, as far as graphics are concerned, is the pixel (short for "picture element" or, in essence, a dot), which can be used to create lines, shapes, and other visual phenomena.

As Joseph Deken writes in *Computer Images: State of the Art* (1983:9):

> The versatility of computer images derives from the active electronic memory and processing systems that support them. While the computer memory-medium can store a direct literal representation of a single image, it can also generate an infinite variety of scenes from an internal computational model.

These computer images, he explains, offer "an entirely new form of visual communication, one that permits the individual viewer to adapt to and interact with the image itself" (1983:9).

For capturing new images, the computer is an instrument of unparalleled reach. Entirely new worlds suddenly come into view: the thermal tides of the human body and the activity of the brain, for example; the geological and biological patterns of the earth's surface; or the radio-wave signatures of objects in space. Like the historic invention of the microscope and telescope, the development of computer-image processing has expanded our vision far beyond the range of the unaided human senses.

JOSEPH DEKEN, *Computer Images: State of the Art*

The secret of the computer's image-making power lies in its ability to store pixels, individual picture elements, and manipulate them. The computer image is a mosaic of pixels, arranged in rows and columns similar to the tiles in a mosaic. Each of these pixels is assigned a location and a predetermined color by the computer, which puts this information into memory and can call it up and manipulate it in innumerable ways, if it is being controlled by the right software.

Software programmers have developed many ingenious products in recent years, and many of the things that used to be done on mainframe or minicomputers can now be done on microcomputers. This applies, especially, to the matter of computer graphics.

The basic elements of a computer system are

1. An input system, such as a keyboard, punched cards, a joystick, or a scanner
2. An output system, such as a printer, a cathode ray tube (familiarly known as a monitor), a plotter, or synthetic speech
3. A peripheral storage system, such as a floppy disk, a hard disk, or magnetic tape
4. Software. There are two kinds: the disk operating software (DOS) that runs the computer and task software, which enables the computer to do various things, such as word processing or creating graphics
5. The computer itself

It was the development of the microprocessor or "computer on a chip" that made it possible to produce inexpensive personal (or micro) computers. Microcomputers can be distinguished from minicomputers, which can cost from around ten thousand dollars to hundreds of thousands of dollars, and mainframe computers, which can cost from hundreds of thousands of dollars to millions of dollars.

In recent years, the price of computers has fallen dramatically. An IBM computer with two disk drives, a twelve-inch monitor, and 640 K of memory cost thousands of dollars in the early 1980s. By 1988, an IBM personal computer (PC) clone with the same power could be had for less than $700. It is necessary to have a powerful personal microcomputer and a hard disk for many graphics uses, but even ordinary personal computers with floppy disks can run many programs.

The development of the Apple Macintosh computer (Figure 8.1) has played a particularly important role as far as graphics are concerned, and the first Macintoshes were sold with a free

graphics program, *Macpaint*, which was extremely easy to use and turned Macintosh users into art directors. *(PageMaker*, the first desktop publishing software program, was originally made for the Mac. It is now available for other kinds of personal computers.) The personal computer industry, for all practical purposes, is divided into two major groups: the IBM-type personal computers, most of which run on a system called MS-DOS (Microsoft Disk Operating System), and the Apple computers, which run on a system Apple has developed. In addition, there are other computers with powerful graphics capabilities, such as the Amiga and the Atari, but these computers have a relatively small market share.

FIGURE 8.1
This photograph shows a Macintosh computer, disk drive, monitor, and printer—what one needs to do word processing and computer graphics.

Graphics Hardware

What follows is a list of some of the more important devices used in personal computer graphics. It is possible to purchase a very inexpensive program that does simple graphics and doesn't use many of the following items, just as it is possible to spend many thousands of dollars to set up a powerful computer graphics system.

Graphics adaptors (cards) These cards affect the resolution of monitors and generate many more pixels per square inch than the computer generates without them. They often generate different type fonts as well. There are many different kinds of graphics adaptors, but a new standard has been developed (though it has not been universally adopted, by any means), the Enhanced Graphics Adaptor (EGA), which can display 16 colors at 640 dots by 350 lines on many monitors. These boards typically cost between $300 and $600.

Light pens These devices enable one to enter information directly into the computer through the use of light. You can literally draw with the pen, and the computer picks up this drawing. Some can be used with touch-screens and others with "point-and-shoot" menus. They are frequently used in computer-assisted design (CAD) and computer-aided design and drafting (CADD) applications and general graphics applications (Figure 8.2). They plug into standard color/graphics adaptors and cost around $200.

FIGURE 8.2
CAD (computer-aided design) drawing, "Memory Card," by Northern Airborne Technology.

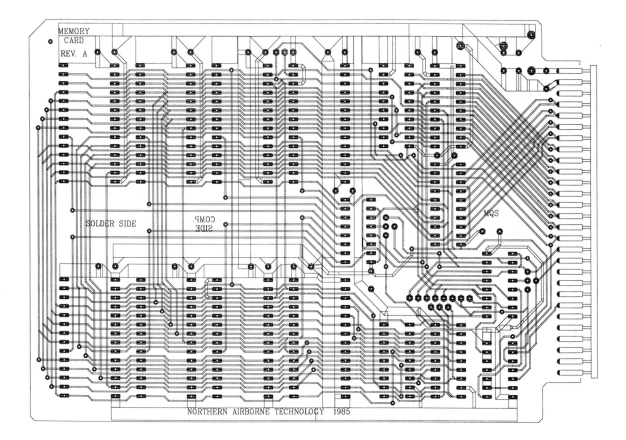

Mice   A mouse is basically a pointing device for computer input and is used in word processing and graphics programs. It is essentially a facilitating device, and many software programs use a mouse to input commands directly (rather than using a keyboard) because of the speed that mice offer. All Macintosh computers come with mice; only about 10 percent of personal computer users have them.

Tablets   These devices often contain large numbers of symbols or commands, which can be put into the computer directly, often with the use of a light pen. They are particularly useful in computer-aided design and drafting programs.

Joysticks   Joysticks are used for direct computer input; they control a cursor or some other aspect of a program. They are often used with video games but can also be used for graphics purposes.

Scanners and optical character readers   These devices enable people to feed images or text directly into a computer. They are extremely useful in desktop publishing and, in fact, threaten to revolutionize all publishing, since they make it unnecessary to keyboard previously written information (articles, books) into computers or typesetting machines.

Plotters   These devices print out charts, graphs, maps, and other graphics, often in many colors.

Printers   Graphics cards enable computers to use regular dot matrix printers to create graphics. The development of the laser printer, which can print three hundred dots per square inch (many times more than the regular dot matrix printer) has facilitated the rise of desktop publishing.

Computer Graphics Software

There are many different kinds of graphics that computers can generate. It all depends on what the user wants to do. For example, there are many inexpensive "print shop" software programs that enable people to make greeting cards, announcements, posters, and drawings. One can purchase "click art" to use with these programs—click art being collections of already drawn images that come in their own programs. (You take an image from the hundreds that are available in the click art program and insert it in your greeting card or announcement with a click of a mouse button or a key on your keyboard.) Frequently you can manipulate this image and make it larger or smaller, to suit your purposes. Some programs enable people to make large signs or banners. There are also so-called "paint" programs that enable people to do animation and to achieve all kinds of special effects with images (Figure 8.3).

One of the most common uses of graphics in the business world is for illustrating reports and other material with charts, tables, and graphs. These charts, tables, and graphs "visualize" data and organize material so that people can make sense of it, very quickly. They show relationships particularly well (Figure 8.4).

FIGURE 8.3
Paint programs. Image (above) was created by Broderbund Software's paint program *Dazzle Draw.* Image (left), by Dominique de Bardonneche-Berglund, was created using *Superpaint* and utilizes the increased power of new computers and advanced software.

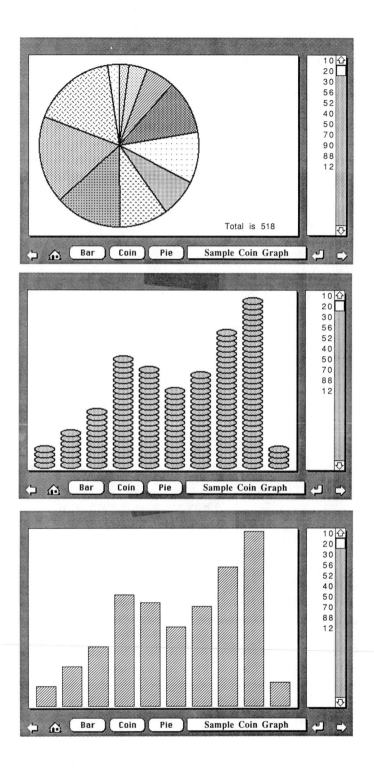

FIGURE 8.4
Charts. These charts were generated on a
Macintosh computer. Charts, graphs, and
diagrams show relationships visually and
thus are able to convey a great deal of
information in an economical manner.

The Nature of the Computer | **163**

Infographics Infographics is a combination of two words—information and graphics—that suggests how strong the relation is between the two phenomena. Much of what we call "information" (statistics and data) is based on relationships. For example, suppose we are told that 50 percent of Americans make $15,000 a year. That piece of information doesn't tell us very much. Is $15,000 a lot or a little? What does this figure mean? (We might think of information as involving data put into some kind of relationship, given a context of some nature.)

If we are told that the 50 percent of American workers get $15,000 and 10 percent get $50,000 and 5 percent get $100,000, and 35 percent get $10,000, we now can place that figure in perspective. But if we are given this information in these words, it takes a good deal of mental work to make sense of the material. Graphics such as charts, pie diagrams, tables, etc., have a unique power to *show* relationships visually. We can see the relationships instantly, instead of having to do mental calculations in our heads.

Examine, for example, Figure 8.5, which shows a great deal of information graphically. Because computers have made creation of charts and diagrams so easy, newspapers and television newscasts are now able to use them regularly.

FIGURE 8.5
Infographics. These simple diagrams convey a great deal of information. Infographics are now found in many newspapers and publications.

Desktop Publishing

Before the development of desktop publishing, organizations that wanted to have good-looking printed materials (reports, brochures, newsletters, etc.) had to rely on artists (to draw pictures, make charts and graphs, and do pasteups) and printers (to set typewritten material into type and print it).

Several things led to the growth of desktop publishing. First, laser printers were developed, which were relatively inexpensive (selling for several thousand dollars) and which offered much better resolution than did conventional dot matrix printers. Second, powerful new software programs, such as *PageMaker* enabled people to integrate and manipulate textual material and visual material with relative ease.

The best desktop publishing software programs have "What You See Is What You Get" (WYSIWYG, as it is popularly known) capabilities. This means people using them can see, on the monitor, exactly what the pages they lay out will look like when they are printed out. These programs allow users to adjust the format of the page, the size of the type fonts, the spacing between characters and lines, and so on. The programs also allow users to "import" texts and graphics generated by other programs and print everything on a laser printer or phototypesetter. It is now possible to purchase a basic desktop publishing system for around $4000, which is very little for any organization that produces very much printed material. A more powerful system can cost several times that much.

The development of desktop publishing means that users can save a great deal of money, since they no longer need pay artists or printers to create reports, newsletters, brochures, booklets — even books. Thus, executives can generate material just the way they want it and not have to wait for anyone else to work on (and perhaps modify) their material. Desktop publishing saves money and it saves time, and it has revolutionized the way individuals and organizations go about creating and publishing material (Figure 8.6).

Computer-Aided Design and Drafting (CADD)

Computers are also an enormous aid to engineers and architects, and the creation of computer-aided design software programs

Brainstorms

Ideas, Opinions, and Speculations from the Mind of Howard Rheingold

Virtual Communities
seem to be one of my themes this year. I wrote about them in my report to the U.S. Congress Office of Technology Assessment, and I wrote an essay about them for next Winter's *Whole Earth Review.* An expansion of the WER piece will appear in *Excursions to the Far side of the Mind*, a book of essays that William Morrow will publish in 1988. Here's a Rheingold's Digest version.

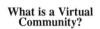

Howard Rheingold
• writes
• edits
• consults

His current books:
• *Tools for Thought*
• *Cognitive Connection*
• *Higher Creativity*

...and more on the way

What is a Virtual Community?

Because I'm a writer, I used to spend my days alone in my room with my words and my thoughts. After work, I would reenter the human community via my neighborhood, my family, my circle of personal and professional acquaintances. But I felt isolated during the working day, and my work provided few opportunities to expand my circle of friends and colleagues. For the past two years, however, I have participated in a wide-ranging, intellectually stimulating, professionally rewarding, and often intensely emotional exchange with dozens of new friends and hundreds of colleagues. And I still spend my days in a room, physically isolated. My mind, however, is linked with a worldwide collection of like-minded (and not so like-minded) souls: My virtual community.

A virtual community is a group of people who may or may not meet one another face to face, and who exchange words and ideas through the mediation of computer bulletin boards and networks. It usually has a geographically local focus and a connection to a much wider domain. The local focus of my virtual community, The Whole Earth 'Lectronic Link (aka "The Well") is the San Francisco Bay Area; the wider locus consists of tens of thousands of other sites around the world, and hundreds of thousands of other people, linked via exchanges of messages into a meta-community known as the Usenet.

The existence of computer-linked communities was predicted twenty years ago by J.C.R. Licklider, who planned the first such community, the ARPAnet: "What will on-line interactive communities be like?" Licklider wrote in 1968: "In most fields they will consist of geographically separated members, sometimes grouped in small clusters and sometimes working individually. They will be communities not of common location, but of common interest..."

My friends and I are part of the future that Licklider dreamed about, and we can attest to the truth of his prediction that "life will be happier for the on-line individual because the people with whom one interacts most strongly will be selected more by commonality of interests and goals than by accidents of proximity."

My community is both a sacred place, in the sense that I visit it for the sheer pleasure of communicating with my friends, and a practical instrument, in the sense that I use it to scan and gather information on subjects that are of momentary or enduring importance, from childcare to neuroscience, technical questions on telecommunications to arguments on philosophical, political, or spiritual subjects. It's a bit like a neighborhood pub or coffee house: Although I don't have to move from my desk, there's a certain sense of place to it. It's a little like a salon, where I can participate in a hundred ongoing

Brainstorms is published by Howard Rheingold • 306 Poplar • Mill Valley, CA • 94941 • (415) 388-3912

FIGURE 8.6
Howard Rheingold, *Brainstorms.* This newsletter was created on a Macintosh computer using a graphics program and a laser printer. Used with permission of Howard Rheingold.

has had an enormous impact on industry. These programs are replacing drafting and designing by hand; they are, in effect, electronic drafting and designing programs that enable architects, engineers, and others to create and manipulate images in remarkable ways. By using various CADD programs, it is possible to generate wire-frame (line) drawings of buildings and devices and then shade them in or render them in color so that you can see what they actually will look like (Figure 8.7). Once a drawing is made and memorized, it can be rotated so that designers can see what it will look like from different angles.

Most programs are pixel-oriented, but some newer ones are object-oriented. They use pixels to create lines and shapes but remember these figures; and when they are enlarged or manipulated, the programs produce sharper images than pixel-oriented ones do.

The most powerful CADD programs cost several thousand dollars, but there are programs with basic CADD capabilities available for as little as $100. (The most dominant CADD software company is Autodesk, whose program *AutoCad* represents about 50 percent of the CADD market and is the industry standard.)

FIGURE 8.7
Diagram of a plane. This image was created using *AutoCad,* the leading computer-aided design and drafting (CADD) software program.

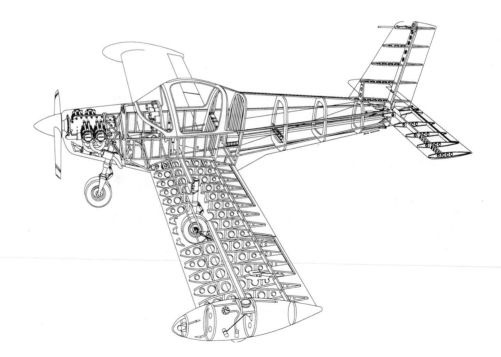

Computer Videogames

The ability of the computer to generate images (and sound) has been an important factor in the development of videogames. The first games such as *Pong*, which appeared in 1972, were very elemental ones that had very little in the way of animation or special effects. In *Pong*, one played table tennis with an electronic blip. As the technology developed and computers became both less expensive and more powerful, computer videogames have become much more elaborate and interesting.

The images are now more realistic; the colors are richer and subtler; there is less distortion; and the games themselves are more complicated and challenging. The quality of the images in these games is affected by the power of the computer it is played on and the capabilities of the monitor being used (Figure 8.8). The same computer game projects different images on different computers and monitors. But even without the most optimal systems, games such as *PacMan* and *Flight Simulator* were able to captivate millions of Americans and achieved incredible popularity.

Special Effects

Many of us do not realize the impact that computers have made on the media. When we watch a television program, many of the things we see (in the beginning, for example, where titles move

FIGURE 8.8
Image from the videogame *Wings of Fury*. This image is typical of those found in computer games. Notice the complexity and realism.

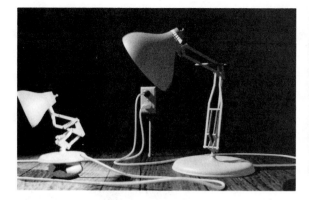 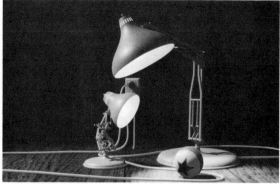

and flip around) are special video effects; commercials use them extensively, also. In addition, video has invaded film and many of the effects we see in movies were generated by video. The science-fiction film *Tron* had more than fifty minutes of video effects in it. And, of course, Music Television (MTV) is full of these video effects.

These effects are created by very powerful computing systems and programs (Figure 8.9). But even the ordinary personal computer, outfitted with a graphics card and using an inexpensive software program, can generate many interesting effects, including some of the following (Figure 8.10):

1. *Mirroring.* Here the computer takes an image and creates a mirror image of it. With some machines, multiple mirror images can be created on one screen and the mirrors can be overlapped if desired.
2. *Mosaic.* This involves the computer's taking an image and mapping squares onto the image that default to the primary color within each square.
3. *Strobe.* Here a freeze effect of an image is held for a short time and released as another is frozen. This stylized effect dramatizes movement within the screen.
4. *Cut and paste.* Video artists can capture sections of an image and place them elsewhere on the image, while manipulating color, shape, and size. In some cases, cutouts can be combined with a live image.
5. *Painting.* A still image is overlaid with color in many different ways, using many different brush techniques to create this effect.
6. *Shattered image.* An image is fractured into slivers or other shapes and shown in this state.

(A)

(B)

(C)

(D)

7. *Posterization.* This process involves increasing image contrast (luminance value) that produces, at the extreme, a cartoon-like quality.

8. *Stenciling.* A shape, regular or irregular, can be created to protect areas of the screen from a given effect; or it can be used in the reverse and dictate where the effect goes.

9. *Chroma-key.* This process electronically takes out red, blue or green from an image and replaces it with a different color or image.

10. *Digitization.* This process puts an image into computer memory for subsequent manipulation.

These are some of the most common effects that can be created by computers. In addition to being used for artistic purposes,

FIGURE 8.10
Bob Malecki, "Special Effects." These special effects were all created by sophisticated computer imaging processes. We see a photograph of a woman and various effects that modify the original image. These images are (A) an unmodified photo of Jan, (B) a mosaic also known as a pixellated image, (C) a solarized or painted image, (D) a frame move repeated with varying degrees of image wash.

computers are also playing an increasingly important role in medicine, where various kinds of imaging processes have been developed. These processes allow physicians to gain valuable information about patients without having to use "intrusive" means (such as exploratory operations). As a result of these new imaging processes, when it is necessary to operate, surgeons have much more precise information on hand before they start the operation.

Conclusions

Have all of the remarkable video effects that computers can generate led to an important new kind of art, or are computer effects essentially one more form of "commercial art," not really a serious art medium? This is a subject of much debate.

Video is still a relatively new medium, so we must give it time to develop and not come to any premature judgments. On the other hand, there has been a great deal of work done in video, so its potentialities should be discernible (Figure 8.11).

FIGURE 8.11
Detail from *Pixellage,* 1983. Choreography by Betty Erickson. Music by A. Corelli. This ballet, appropriately named, used computer-generated images to create remarkable effects.

Michael Noll, who was one of the earliest people to write about the subject, expressed a great deal of optimism about the medium in an essay, "Computers and The Visual Arts," written in 1967. He wrote:

> In the computer, man has created not just an inanimate tool but an intellectual and active creative partner that, when fully exploited, could be used to produce wholly new art forms and possibly new aesthetic experiences.

By 1982, Noll had serious reservations. As he wrote (in the catalog of a SIGGRAPH [Special Interest Group on Computer Graphics] art show):

> It is in its use as a serious artistic medium in the visual arts where the digital computer has not yet achieved its anticipated potential. Digital computers are being used to create visual imagery, but many people feel that something is missing.
>
> The images sometimes appear to be attempts to mimic other media. Many are cold and sterile and are somewhat devoid of human expression. Randomness combines with geometric structure to create designs that are frequently interesting but that are little more. One is frequently left with the impression that many patterns are simply experiments in learning the new medium.

Noll raises the question as to whether there is some kind of fundamental antithesis between technology and the arts, between machines and what might be called "the human spirit" (Figure 8.12).

FIGURE 8.12
(A) Michael Noll, *Computer Composition with Lines,* 1964. (B) P. Mondrian, *Composition with Lines,* 1917. The computer-generated image (A) was created to be very similar to (B), Mondrian's work. When Noll showed audiences the two images, labeling them "A" and "B," and asked which was the Mondrian, large percentages thought that the computer-generated image (A) was the Mondrian. This occurred because, it is hypothesized, the computer-generated image was more irregular or random than the Mondrian painting. Another of Mondrian's paintings, *Composition with Blue and Yellow,* is shown in Figure 0.6.

(A)

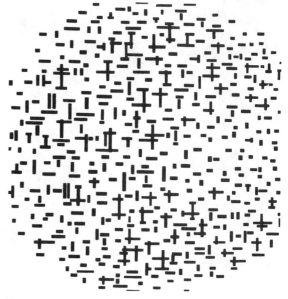

(B)

What will happen with video remains to be seen. There are serious video artists, who are experimenting with video and trying to create works of significance. But how different is their work from film, except for the greater use of special effects? Or television?

The future will tell us what to make of computer art and video. For the moment, computers enable people to create and manipulate images of all sorts in remarkable ways. Whether this technology will develop into a "serious" art that creates ennobling works of lasting quality remains to be seen.

Applications

1. What impact do you think computers have had on society? (If you have a computer, what effect has it had on your life?) Be as specific as you can in answering this question.

2. In what ways have computers directly impacted on your life? Make a list of particulars and briefly explain each item. You might take one day in your life and see where and how computers are involved with your activities, either directly or indirectly.

3. Newspapers often run stories about young students, known as "hackers," who use their computers to get into the computer systems of the Army or other large organizations. What do you think motivates these hackers? What should be done to hackers who are caught?

4. If you have access to a computer, use it to make a newsletter that you will give to your friends. Decide on its title and what it will look like. If you don't have a desktop publishing program, you can make a pasteup with printed matter from the computer and art work you do by hand.

5. If you have access to a computer, play some games on it for an hour. Write a short essay describing what the experience was like.

6. Play sociologist. Go to a videogame arcade and survey the players. What questions should you ask them? Make sure some of the questions involve obtaining quantitative data. When you are done, examine the data and write a report describing what you found and explaining what it means.

7. Watch *Tron,* which contains almost an hour of computer animation. Write a review of the film, focusing on its aesthetic aspects.

Glossary

A to B axis : The axis that goes from the left side of a screen to the right side. (See Z-axis.)

Aesthetics The branch of philosophy concerned with questions related to the nature of the beautiful: what is the relation between truth and beauty, between form and content, etc. Applied aesthetics, in contrast, is interested in how to obtain certain effects through the use of color, lighting, certain camera shots, editing, etc.

Auto-eroticism In aesthetics, sensual pleasure caused by contemplation of one's image.

Axial balance Formal balance in which elements in a visual field are arranged symmetrically on both sides of an axis.

Balance The arrangement of elements in a visual field that produces a sense of order and stability.

Bicameral brain The two hemispheres of the brain, each of which has certain characteristics. The left hemisphere is associated with logic and is linear; the right hemisphere is associated with imagination and is holistic.

CAD (computer-aided design) Software programs that enable users such as architects and engineers to create designs on computers and manipulate the images for various purposes. There are now CADD (computer-aided design and drafting) programs as well, for draftspersons and others.

Caricature A form of humorous drawing that captures the likeness of a person but exaggerates and distorts various features of that person.

Cartoon A drawing, usually in one frame, depicting some kind of humorous situation, which is generally accompanied by a caption.

Chart A means of presenting information in visual form so that relationships can immediately be seen.

Chiaroscuro lighting A form of lighting characterized by very strong lights and darks, as opposed to flat lighting, which diminishes the differences between lights and darks.

Click art Software programs that contain drawings and other visual phenomena that can be used in preparing newsletters, reports, and any other kind of desktop publishing.

Close-up A term used to describe a film or television camera shot that shows a person's head. There are also extreme close-ups, which show only part of a person's face. Many people suggest that because of its small screen size, television is a close-up medium.

Codes Ways of interpreting signs and symbols and organizing behavior. There are highway codes, which are known and which people are tested on, and aesthetic codes, which often escape our awareness but also often shape our behavior.

Color The description we use for things based on the way light is reflected or emitted from objects. Colors are differentiated in terms of hue, saturation, and brightness. We also distinguish between primary colors, red, yellow and blue, and secondary colors, orange, green, purple, etc.

Colorization The capacity of certain computers and software programs to modify the colors in images. As a result of this process, black-and-white films and television programs can be turned into color, though there is a great deal of dispute about the propriety of doing so.

Comic strip A popular art form, generally found in newspapers, characterized by having continuing characters, a number of panels, and dialogue presented in balloons. Comic strips can be either serious or humorous, and often are extremely long-lived.

Composition The arrangement of elements in a visual field so as to please the eye or obtain an intended effect.

Condensation The psychological process by which the mind unifies and pulls together disparate images in dreams so as to avoid the dream censor. The condensed image generally has a sexual dimension to it, though this is not apparent. We also react to the sexual content of condensed images when we are awake, though we do not create these images.

Contrast A difference between two visual elements (such as simple and complicated, dull and bright, or dark and light) to generate emphasis and display.

Cool medium One that provides relatively few data and thus generates strong involvement on the part of the viewer or listener. A **hot medium** is just the opposite.

Depth of field The capacity of a camera to keep objects, located at different distances from it, in focus. Depth of field can vary, based on the f-stop of the camera, the focal length of the lens, and the distance from the camera to the object being photographed.

Desktop publishing The use of computers, powerful software programs that enable users to manipulate textual and visual material, and laser printers to produce high-quality printed matter (such as reports, pamphlets, books, etc.).

Digitized image An image put into a computer that can then be manipulated for various purposes.

Direction The line of movement of some aspect of an image. These directions are sometimes known as vectors.

Displacement The psychological process by which the mind invests an object or symbol with significance taken from some other object or symbol. Frequently this significance has a sexual dimension to it, and the displaced objects often are similar (in shape or function) to the object that is displaced.

Dot A small, round mark. Dots are made by the intersection of two lines. Computers generate dots (on monitors) that are called pixels.

Dot-matrix printer A kind of printer, used with computers, that uses dots to form letters and other visual material. The typical dot-matrix printer generates 75 dots per inch in contrast to the laser printer, which produces 300 dots per inch.

Drama A narrative or story, usually involving strong emotions and conflict among or between characters and the resolution of the conflict by action.

Editing The editing process in film or television takes place after images have been taken by a camera. Editing involves putting together the various elements or components of a film or television program in a manner that produces the impact and effect desired. This often involves cutting (eliminating) some material, and splicing bits and pieces together. Editing is often done manually in films, but new devices have been developed that enable the editing process to be done electronically.

Figure-ground A relationship between an object and the background against which we see the object. The background affects the meaning figures have, since they often are ambiguous.

Film frame The basic unit of a film is the frame, which is, in essence, a photographic negative of a static image. Film is projected at twenty-four frames per second, which—because of a visual phenomenon known as an afterimage—produces the illusion of movement.

Flat lighting Lighting in which differences between lights and darks are minimized or flattened. The opposite of *chiaroscuro* lighting.

Flipping The process of using a remote-control tuner to "flip" from one television station to another, which means people flipping do not watch programs but, instead, create their own programs from bits and pieces of what is on the air.

Flush left Lining type up in a straight line on the left margin of a page. Flush right involves lining it up in a straight line on the right margin of a page. Textual matter in books and magazines is generally flush left and flush right or "justified." Ragged right, in which lines do not line up in a straight line, is held by many typographers to give a more modern or contemporary look to a page.

Focus The clarity or sharpness of an image. Soft focus generates images that are not precise and clear and produces a dream-like effect.

Freeze-frame The capacity of computers using certain software programs to capture an image and keep it immobile. It is maintained as if it has been frozen. Freeze-frame is also used in film to suggest arrested motion and generate a feeling of surprise or shock.

Genre This term refers to kinds of stories, programs, or films. We make a distinction between a medium (film, television, etc.) and the kind of programs or genres it carries: soap operas, quiz shows, sports shows, interview shows, news shows, documentaries, etc.

Gestalt The psychological process by which we combine a number of disparate elements into a whole that is greater than the sum of its parts and whose properties cannot be derived from the various parts. We commonly use the term to mean "putting things together" and getting some kind of an insight.

Glamorization The process by which we invest people or objects with qualities that we find appealing and desirable. A photographer can glamorize through the use of lighting, background, camera angles, and filtering devices.

Graph A form of visual display showing quantitative relationships, often in the form of bars or points on a field.

Grid layout A collection of crisscrossing lines that make simple forms. These grid forms are used to help people without much knowledge of design format visual material in an attractive manner and avoid mistakes. Some desktop publishing software programs come with grids in them and include advice about good layout.

Illustration The use of drawings, paintings or other visual material to exemplify, give focus to, or decorate textual material.

Image A visual representation of something or someone. Images can be thought of as being complex pictorial phenomena, often having symbolic significance and unconscious meanings. Image also refers to the concept we have about someone or something.

Imagination Ability of the mind to create new ideas, images, etc., or to visualize things not present. The term suggests there is a link between images or visual phenomena and creative behavior.

Index Signs are indexical when they signify by logic or causal connection, as in the case of smoke and fire.

Information overload A numbness and inability to process information caused by overexposure to it.

Intertextuality Commonly understood to deal with the fact that works in the arts (or "texts" in the language of semiotics) often borrow from or are related in various ways to other texts. For example, a parody imitates and makes fun of another work.

Jump cut A quick cut from one scene to another that leaves out some intermediate scenes and thus speeds the action.

Laser printer A printer, commonly used in desktop publishing, which offers relatively high resolution—300 dots per square inch.

Layout See *composition.*

Logo A design, sometimes made of letters, used by an organization as a means of establishing its identity.

Metaphor A figure of speech indicating an analogy or similarity between two things. Example: My love is a rose. (See *simile.*)

Metonymy A method of generating meaning through the use of association. Example: a mansion suggests wealth (and good taste).

Montage A series of images and sounds that, when combined in a certain way, generate a powerful effect.

Mosaic A form of pictorial representation in which an image is created out of small, colored pieces of stone or some other material. This effect can also be created by computers with the right imaging software.

Movement A sense of activity or change in position. It is created in films and television by the actions of characters and in static visual fields by use of line, shape, lighting, and color.

Music television (MTV) Videos, generally performed by music groups, which either dramatize a song or show it being performed. Many of these videos use avant-garde film techniques.

Narcotization A sense of deadness and boredom created, for example, by watching too much television, which can prevent the alternating of left-brain and right-brain activity.

Optical illusion A visual image that confuses the viewer and is deceptive.

Persistence of vision The process that enables us to connect the frames of a film and "see" the film as continuous.

Perspective The ability to represent three-dimensional objects and give a sense of depth on a two-dimensional plane.

Phallic symbol Any object that, for one reason or another, such as resemblance in shape or similarity in function, suggests the male sexual organ.

Pica A unit of measurement in type equivalent to 12 points or approximately one-sixth inch.

Pixel An abbreviation of "picture element." Essentially a point or dot that is shown on a computer monitor and that is the building block out of which lines, shapes, and images are created.

Plotter A printing device used to reproduce drawings, architectural renderings, and other visual phenomena using computers and graphics software programs.

Point A unit of measurement in typography equal to approximately 1/72 inch. Twelve points make a pica.

Pose To assume a particular posture for a portrait or photograph that reflects feelings and attitudes and generates a desired image.

Proportion A relationship between elements in a visual field in which a part is considered with respect to the whole.

Psyche The mind in all its conscious and unconscious functions and capacities, as a center of intellectual thought, emotions, and behavior. Freud suggested the psyche is made up of an id (drives), a superego (conscience), and an ego (rationality) that mediates between the id and superego, two opposing forces.

Psychological closure The way the mind combines elements into wholes and completes visual phenomena that are incomplete.

Reaction shot A television shot showing a person's reactions (by facial expression) to some event. These shots generate a sense of drama and excitement.

Reverse print Having white type on a black background (or some variation on that theme) instead of the usual black type on a white background.

Roman typeface A typeface characterized by upright letters, lines of varying thicknesses, and serifs.

Saccades The quick, intermittent movements the eye makes when it fixes on one point after another in a visual field. Each saccade lasts approximately 1/20 second.

Sans serif typeface A typeface without serifs, the little marks that finish off the main strokes of letters in certain typefaces.

Scale A relationship of size between objects or elements in a visual field.

Scanner A device that can input graphics or textual material directly into a computer.

Selective perception The process by which people tend to see only certain things in a given situation. They focus on material of interest to them and neglect other things that are present.

Semiotics The science of signs that investigates the way meaning is produced and transmitted. (See *sign*.)

Shape The visible configuration or outward form of something.

Shattered image An image, broken into pieces to achieve a desired aesthetic effect, through the use of computers and imaging software programs.

Shot angle The angle at which a photo, film, or television shot is taken, used to promote an effect or feeling in the viewer.

Sign One of the basic concepts of semiotics. A sign is anything that can be used to stand for something else. Words, images, facial expression, clothing, hairstyles — just about everything can be seen as a sign. How signs work and problems connected with signs are the subject matter of semiotics.

Signifier/signified According to Ferdinand de Saussure, signs are divided into signifiers (sounds or objects) and signifieds (the concepts generated by the signifier). The relation between signifiers and signifieds is arbitrary or conventional.

Simile A figure of speech, using "like" or "as," in which a weak relationship between two subjects is posited. "My love is like a rose." (See *metaphor.*)

Sound effects The use of made-up sounds or noises (generally in dramatic presentations) to simulate real sounds and noises and generate emotional responses and a sense of verisimilitude in those who hear them.

Spatiality The sense of space, determined in large part by the amount of "white" space, in a visual field.

Strobe A special effect characterized by short, bright pulses of light, turning on and off.

Supergraphics Use of letters and words and other visual phenomena on a very large scale.

Surrealism A twentieth-century artistic (and literary) movement that attempted to capture the working of the subconscious by using fantastic imagery and trying to approximate a dreamlike state.

Symbol A form of sign, for Peirce, in which the meaning is conventional and must be learned. In ordinary use, anything that stands for something else, often on the basis of convention or association.

Table A visual means of presenting numerical relationships among data, generally in columns and rows.

Talking heads Television programs in which there is little physical action and basically nothing but conversation takes place are said to be "talking heads" programs.

Typography The art of selecting and using typefaces for maximum effect. It also involves such matters as the composition of the page and the sizing of illustrations and other graphics.

Unity A sense of harmoniousness and wholeness created by the relationships of elements in a visual field.

WYSIWYG (What You See Is What You Get) The ability of certain software programs to provide users with an accurate picture of what a page will look like when it is printed out. This feature is of particular importance in desktop publishing.

Z-axis shot A shot in which the action is vertical to the screen image and moves toward or away from the viewer. This kind of shot is particularly important in television since the screen is so small.

Zoom shot A shot in which the lens of a camera is used to move in on a scene for a closer view (or, in the reverse, move away from a scene). If used too frequently, zoom shots lose their impact and disturb viewers.

Selected Annotated Bibliography

The literature on visual communication is vast. There are an incredible number of books on aesthetics, art, design, graphics, film, television, and related concerns. And with good reason, for if we are "thinking creatures" (homo sapiens) we are also "seeing creatures" (homo oculans). What follows is a listing and brief description of some of the more important and interesting books in the field. A more complete listing of books (including those cited in the text) follows in the References.

Berger, Arthur Asa. *Li'l Abner: A Study in American Satire.* 1970. Twayne Publishers.
This study deals with the social, cultural, and political significance of one of America's most important comic strips, Li'l Abner. It considers such topics as comics and popular culture, satire, and graphic techniques in the comics.

Berger, Arthur Asa. *The Comic-Stripped American: What Dick Tracy, Blondie, Daddy Warbucks and Charlie Brown Tell Us About Ourselves.* 1973. Walker & Co.
This book analyzes the cultural and symbolic significance of many of America's classic comic strips.

Berger, Arthur Asa. *Signs in Contemporary Culture: An Introduction to Semiotics.* 1984. Longman.
This book explains some of the basic concepts of semiotic theory and applies them to various topics, many of which involve visual matters.

Berger, John. *Ways of Seeing.* 1972. Penguin Books.
This book is based on a series of four television broadcasts that the English critic, John Berger, made for the BBC. It has four written essays (on images, the portrayal of women in art, politics and art, and advertising) and three pictorial ones.

Berger, John. *About Looking.* 1980. Pantheon.
This is a collection of essays that previously appeared in an English magazine, New Society. The essays deal with such matters as why we look at animals, how we use photography, and the significance of various artists and works of art.

Clark, Kenneth. *Looking at Pictures.* 1968. Beacon Press.
This book contains a number of analyses by Clark that are meant to teach us how to look at paintings in as profound and discerning a manner as possible. Clark argues that knowing about a painter's life, his personality, his beliefs and values, where the painting fits into a painter's total work, and what the art of his time was like, are necessary to interpret a given work and look at pictures (in general) correctly.

Deken, Joseph. *Computer Images: State of the Art.* 1983. Stewart, Tabori & Chang.
This book is full of remarkable four-color images generated by computers. It deals with computers and images, how the computer is affecting our aesthetic sensibilities, the role of computer images and fantasy, and related topics.

Dichter, Ernest. *Packaging: The Sixth Sense? A Guide to Identifying Consumer Motivation.* 1975. Cahners Publishing.
Dichter, the father of motivation research, deals with the power of packaging and shows how it is involved with deep-seated psychological anxieties we all experience. Much interesting material on how people interpret symbols and relate to visual phenomena, especially as these matters apply to packaging and "commercial communication."

Dondis, Donis A. *A Primer of Visual Literacy.* 1973. MIT Press.
This is an early textbook on visual communication that deals with what visual literacy is, composition, visual techniques, how the visual arts function, and similar topics. It contains numerous line drawings and other illustrations and offers a good introduction to the principles of design.

Eisenstein, Sergei. *Film Form: Essays in Film Theory.* Edited and translated by Jay Leyda. 1949. Harcourt Brace Jovanovich.
A series of essays on various aspects of film theory by a famous film director. Eisenstein deals with such topics as the nature of film form, film language, montage, and the structure of film. A companion book of essays, Film Sense, is available from the same publisher.

Foucault, Michel. *This is Not a Pipe.* 1983. University of California Press.
This fascinating little book deals with the work of the Belgian Surrealist, René Magritte. One of his most famous paintings shows a pipe and underneath it is written "this is not a pipe." Foucault attempts to explain what Magritte's visual non sequiturs mean.

Gowans, Alan. *The Unchanging Arts: New Forms for the Traditional Functions of Art in Society.* 1971. J. B. Lippincott.
Gowans deals with the functions of art in society and covers everything from the arts of antiquity to advertising and comic strips. His scope is incredible and his insights are astounding.

Gowans, Alan. *Learning To See: Historical Perspective on Modern Popular/Commercial Arts.* 1981. Bowling Green University Popular Press.
This book carries forward the arguments of The Unchanging Arts *and updates it. Gowans deals with everything from Chinese Junks to soap operas and football. Provocative and fascinating.*

Grotjahn, Martin. *The Voice of the Symbol.* 1971. Delta Books.
This book provides a Freudian psychoanalytic interpretation of many of our most important symbols — and deals with such topics as television, dreams, and the work of Hieronymus Bosch.

Jung, Carl G. (ed.) *Man and his Symbols.* 1964. Dell Books.
Articles by Jung and his followers on the relation between the symbol and the psyche, with much material on art and other forms of visual communication. Jung elaborated a different psychology from Freud, and it is instructive to see how Jungians analyze things. Profusely illustrated.

Kris, Ernst. *Psychoanalytic Explorations in Art.* 1964. Schocken Books.
This collection of essays by Kris (sometimes collaborating with other authors) applies psychoanalytic theory to expressive behavior. It has chapters on art and psychoanalysis, the art of the insane, caricature, and the creative process.

Kurtz, Bruce. *Spots: The Popular Art of American Television Commercials.* 1977. Arts Communications.
Written to provide readers with a conceptual framework to understand television commercials. Shows how commercials work, how they relate to (and borrow from) other works and media. Has interviews with some important makers of commercials and analyses of their work.

Sontag, Susan. *On Photography.* 1973. Delta Books.
A series of philosophical essays on the nature of photography, its relation to other art forms, and its social and political significance. Also discusses the work of many important photographers. Originally written as a series of essays for The New York Review of Books. *A provocative and illuminating book.*

Ude-Pestel, Anneliese. *Betty: History and Art of a Child in Therapy.* 1977. Science and Behavior Books.
This fascinating book deals with a terribly disturbed child and her paintings and drawings. Her art shows the way she progresses and moves from terrifying images of a person in great pain to images one might expect from a little girl. The book contains 26 paintings by Betty that show how she changes as the result of her therapy.

Worth, Sol. *Studying Visual Communication.* Edited, with an introduction by Larry Gross. 1981. University of Pennsylvania Press.
This is a collection of scholarly essays by a film maker and theorist of visual communication. The essays deal with topics such as the semiotics of film, the nature and functions of symbolism, and the uses of film in education.

Zettl, Herbert. *Sight, Sound, Motion: Applied Media Aesthetics.* 1973. Wadsworth Publishing Company.
A pioneering work, encyclopedic in nature, on the principles of aesthetics, with particular reference to film and television. Zettl shows how important a role aesthetic matters — light, color, sound, camera work, etc. — play in the media. Lavishly illustrated.

References

Albers, Joseph. 1971. *Interaction of Color.* New Haven: Yale University Press.

Arnheim, Rudolf. 1953. *Film as Art.* Berkeley: University of California Press.

Arnheim, Rudolf. 1966. *Toward a Psychology of Art.* Berkeley: University of California Press.

Arnheim, Rudolf. 1969. *Visual Thinking.* London: Faber & Faber.

Barthes, Roland. 1957. *Mythologies.* New York: Hill & Wang.

Bassett, Richard. 1969. *The Open Eye in Learning.* Cambridge: M.I.T. Press.

Becker, Howard S. 1982. *Art Worlds.* Berkeley: University of California Press.

Behrens, Roy R. 1984. *Design in the Visual Arts.* Englewood Cliffs, N.J.: Prentice-Hall.

Berger, Arthur Asa. 1976. *The Comic-Stripped American.* New York: Walker & Co.

Berger, Arthur Asa. 1982. *Media Analysis Techniques.* Beverly Hills: Sage.

Berger, Arthur Asa. 1984. *Signs in Contemporary Culture.* New York: Longmans.

Berger, John. 1972. *Ways of Seeing.* New York: Penguin.

Berger, John. 1988. *About Looking.* New York: Pantheon.

Boggs, Joseph M. 1978. *The Art of Watching Films.* Menlo Park, Calif.: Benjamin/Cummings.

Bronowski, J. 1978. *The Visionary Eye.* Cambridge: M.I.T. Press.

Bullen, J. B. 1981. *Vision & Design.* London: Oxford University Press.

Clark, Kenneth. 1960. *Looking at Pictures.* Boston: Beacon Press.

Collier, John. 1967. *Visual Anthropology.* New York: Holt, Rinehart and Winston.

Curtiss, Deborah. 1987. *Introduction to Visual Literacy.* Englewood Cliffs, N.J.: Prentice-Hall.

Deken, Joseph. 1983. *Computer Images: State of the Art.* New York: Stewart, Tabori & Chang.

Dondis, Donis. 1973. *A Primer of Visual Literacy.* Cambridge: M.I.T. Press.

Edwards, Betty. 1979. *Drawing on the Right Side of the Brain.* Los Angeles: J. P. Tarcher.

Edwards, Betty. 1986. *Drawing on the Artist Within.* New York: Simon & Schuster.

Eisenstein, Sergei. 1942. *The Film Sense.* New York: Harvest/HBJ.

Eisenstein, Sergei. 1949. *Film Form.* New York: Harvest/HBJ.

Eisner, Elliot W. 1972. *Educating Artistic Vision.* New York: Macmillan.

Esslin, Martin. 1982. *The Age of Television.* San Francisco. W. H. Freeman.

Feldman, Edmund Burke. 1973. *Varieties of Visual Experience.* New York: Abrams.

Fransecky, R. B., and Debes, John L. 1972. *Visual Literacy.* Washington, D. C.: Association for Educational Communication.

Gattegno, Caleb. 1969. *Towards a Visual Culture.* New York: Avon.

Gombrich, E. H. 1961. *Art and Illusion.* New York: Pantheon.

Gotschalk, D. W. 1947. *Art and the Social Order.* New York: Dover.

Gowans, Alan. 1971. *The Unchanging Arts: New Forms for the Traditional Functions of Art in Society.* Philadelphia: Lippincott.

Gowans, Alan. 1981. *Learning to See.* Bowling Green, Ohio: Bowling Green University.

Hanks, Kurt, et al. 1978. *Design Yourself.* Los Altos, Calif.: Kaufmann.

Hanson, Jarice. 1987. *Understanding Video.* Newbury Park, Calif.: Sage.

Hogg, James, ed. 1970. *Psychology and the Visual Arts.* Baltimore: Penguin.

Huxley, Aldous. 1942. *The Art of Seeing.* New York: Harper.

Jung, Carl, ed. 1964. *Man and His Symbols.* New York: Doubleday.

Jussim, Estelle. 1974. *Visual Communication and the Graphic Arts.* New York: Bowker.

Kepes, Gyorgy. 1944. *Language of Vision.* Chicago: Paul Theobald.

Kepes, Gyorgy. 1965. *Education of Vision.* New York: Braziller.

Kris, Ernst. 1964. *Psychoanalytic Explorations in Art.* New York: Schocken.

Lieberman, J. Ben. 1968. *Types of Typefaces.* New York: Sterling.

Lindstrom, Miriam. 1962. *Children's Art.* Berkeley: University of California Press.

McKim, Robert H. 1980. *Thinking Visually.* Belmont, Calif.: Wadsworth.

McLuhan, Marshall. 1965. *Understanding Media: The Extensions of Man.* New York: McGraw-Hill.

Mehrabian, Albert. 1971. *Silent Messages.* Belmont, Calif.: Wadsworth.

Moholy-Nagy, Laszlo. 1947. *Vision in Motion.* Chicago: Paul Theobald.

Monaco, James. 1977. *How to Read a Film.* New York: Oxford University Press.

Noll, A. Michael. 1967. "Computers and the Visual Arts. *Design and Planning #2,* New York: Hastings House.

Noll, A. Michael. 1982. Catalogue of SIGGRAPH Art Show.

Novitz, David. 1977. *Pictures and Their Use in Communication.* The Hague: Martinus Nijhoff.

Ornstein, Robert. 1972. *The Psychology of Consciousness.* San Francisco: W. H. Freeman.

Paivio, Allan. 1979. *Imagery and Verbal Processes.* Hillsdale, N. J.: Lawrence Erlbaum Associates.

Preble, Duane and Sarah. 1985. *Artforms.* New York: Harper & Row.

Pryluck, Calvin. 1976. *Sources of Meaning in Motion Pictures & Television.* New York: Arno Press.

Reitberger, Rheinhold, and Fuchs, Wolfgang. 1972. *Comics: Anatomy of a Mass Medium.* Boston: Little, Brown & Company.

Saussure, Ferdinand de. 1966. *Course in General Linguistics.* New York: McGraw-Hill.

Schwartz, Tony. 1974. *The Responsive Chord.* New York: Doubleday.

Sebeok, Thomas A. 1979. *The Sign and Its Masters.* Austin: The University of Texas Press.

Sontag, Susan. 1966. *Against Interpretation.* New York: Farrar, Straus & Giroux.

Sontag, Susan. 1973. *On Photography.* New York: Farrar, Straus & Giroux.

Stern, Raphael and Ester. 1983. *Changing Concepts of Art.* New York: Haven Publications.

Taylor, Joshua C. 1975. *To See Is To Think: Looking at American Art.* Washington, D. C.: Smithsonian Institution.

Wileman, R. E. 1980. *Exercises in Visual Thinking.* New York: Hastings House.

Worth, Sol. 1981. *Studying Visual Communication.* Philadelphia: University of Pennsylvania Press.

Youngblood, Gene. 1970. *Expanded Cinema.* New York: Dutton.

Zettl, Herbert. 1973. *Sight, Sound, Motion.* Belmont, Calif.: Wadsworth.

Illustration Credits

All illustrations not otherwise credited have been provided by the author.

Introduction

0.3, 0.4, 0.5 Courtesy of Annaliese Ude-Pestel, author of *Betty: History and Art of a Child in Therapy.*

0.6 Courtesy of The Hirshhorn Museum and Sculpture Garden, Smithsonian Institution, Washington, D. C. Gift of Joseph H. Hirshhorn, 1972.

0.7 Courtesy of Apple Computer, Inc. and Chiat/Day Advertising.

0.8 Courtesy of Cosmair, Inc.

0.9 © Pixar. All rights reserved.

0.10 Courtesy of The National Archives, Washington, D. C.

0.11, 0.12 Jason Berger

0.13, 0.14 Courtesy of National Portrait Gallery, Smithsonian Institution, Washington, D. C.

0.15 Reproduced by permission of Varityper Corporation.

0.16 *(left)* Drawing by M. C. Escher. Used by permission. © M. C. Escher Heirs in c/o Cordon Art-Baam-Holland. *(right)* Art Resource

0.17 Leonard Freed, Magnum

0.18 Used with permission of the Hirshhorn Museum and Sculpture Garden, Smithsonian Institution, Washington, D. C. Gift of Joseph H. Hirshhorn Foundation, 1972.

0.19 *(p. 12 and top of p. 13)* From *Signs, Symbols & Ornaments* by Rene Smeets. © 1975, 1982 by Van Nostrand Reinhold Company. Reprinted by permission. *(bottom p. 13)* Reprinted with permission of Apple Computer Company.

0.20 From *The Complete Grimm's Fairytales* by The Brothers Grimm, translated by Margaret Hunt and James Stern. Illustrated by Josef Scharl. Copyright 1944 by Pantheon Books, Inc. and renewed 1972 by Random House, Inc. Reprinted by permission of the publisher.

0.21 Detail from Bosch, *Temptation of St. Anthony.* Art Resource.

0.22 © 1987 New World Pictures. All rights reserved. Provided by PhotoEdit.

Chapter 1

1.1 © Bill Owens, Jeroboam, Inc.

1.2 Ally & Gargano Advertising. Art Director, Ron Arnold. Copywriter, Tom Messner.

1.4 Foote, Cone & Belding Advertising. Reproduced courtesy of Levi Strauss & Co.

1.5 Illustration by Lorelle Raboni in "Eye Movements and Visual Perception" by David Norton and Lawrence Stark, SCIENTIFIC AMERICAN, June 1971, p. 37, bottom.

1.6 Used with permission of the Hirshhorn Museum and Sculpture Garden, Smithsonian Institution, Washington, D. C. Gift of Joseph H. Hirshhorn Foundation, 1966.

Chapter 2

2.8 Courtesy of Landor Associates and General Motors Corporation.

2.9 Courtesy of Landor Associates and Black & Decker, Inc.

2.12 (a) AP/Wide World, (b) © Sanford Roth, Photo Researchers.

2.14 Reprinted with permission of Smith/Greenland, Inc.

2.16 © Jerry Uelsmann.

2.18 Courtesy of Bob Malecki and Island Graphics Corp.

2.19 Art Resource.

2.26 Courtesy of Safeway Stores, Inc.

2.27 Used courtesy of Gumps, Inc.

2.28, 2.29 Used by permission of Hal Riney & Partners, San Francisco, California.

2.30 Costa Manos, Magnum.

2.32 © Arnold Newman.

2.33 © Erich Hartmann, Magnum.

2.34 Art Resource.

2.36 Reprinted with permission of Smith/Greenland, Inc.

2.37 © Charles Harbutt, Archive.

2.38 Reproduced courtesy of the Philbrook Art Museum, Tulsa, Oklahoma.

Chapter 3

3.1, 3.2, 3.14, 3.15, 3.16 Used by permission of the White House.

3.3 (a) © George Holton, Photo Researchers, (b) © Dennis Carlyle Darling.

3.4, 3.5, 3.9 Reproduced by permission of *Studies in Visual Communication,* a journal devoted to visual anthropology.

3.6 Photo by Nicole Bengiveno. Used by permission of the San Francisco Ballet.

3.7, 3.8 AP/Wide World Photos.

3.10, 3.11 Courtesy of Bob Malecki and Island Graphics Corp.

3.12 (a) © Bill Burke, Archive (b) © Karsh, Ottawa. Woodfin Camp & Associates.

3.13 (a) © Arnold Newman; (b) Vernon Meritt III, Life Magazine, © 1962; (c) © Peter Buckley, Bullfight Critic, Logrono, 1956. (1956) Gelatin-silver print, 19 × 15½ inches. Collection, The Museum of Modern Art, New York. Gift of the photographer.

3.17 © Evan Johnson, Jeroboam.

3.18 © Ansel Adams. Reproduced courtesy of the National Archives.

3.19 Photos by Richard Noble. © Time, Inc. Reprinted with permission.

3.20 Hirshhorn Museum and Sculpture Garden, Smithsonian Institute. Purchased from Allan Frumkin Gallery, 1985.

Chapter 4

4.1, 4.2, 4.4, 4.6, 4.9 Museum of Modern Art/Film Stills Archives.

4.5 Used with permission of Gilbert Shelton.

4.7 *Mr. Smith Goes to Washington* courtesy Columbia Pictures Corp.

4.8 *Rocky,* © 1976 United Artists Corp.

4.9 *Raiders of the Lost Ark,* courtesy Paramount Pictures Corp.

4.10 *The Seventh Seal,* courtesy Janus Films.

Chapter 5

5.4 © Lee Friedlander. Galax, Virginia. (1962) Gelatin-silver print, 5⅞ × 8⅞ inches. Collection, The Museum of Modern Art, New York. Gift of Mrs. Armand P. Bartos.

5.7 Reproduced with permission of Levi Strauss & Company.

5.8 Reproduced by permission of Apple Computer, Inc.

5.9, 5.10, 5.11 Reproduced by permission of Lynn Hershman.

Chapter 6

6.1 © 1950, 1954, 1956 United Features Syndicate.

6.2, 6.4, 6.8 Reproduced by permission of Universal Press Syndicate.

6.3 Reprinted by permission: Tribune Media Services.

6.5, 6.13 Used with permission of Hal Riney & Partners, San Francisco, California.

6.14 Chris Van Dusen, ''Happy Birthday, Mom.'' © The Main Line Company, Rockport, ME. Used with permission.

Chapter 7

7.1 Photograph by David Powers. Used with permission.

7.2, 7.4, 7.7 Reprinted with permission of *U&lc, International Journal of Typographics.*

7.3 From Rookledge's International Typefinder. Reproduced with kind permission of Sarema Press (Publishers) Limited of London, England.

7.5 Courtesy Brenda Booth.

7.6 Used with permission of Hal Riney & Partners, San Francisco, California.

7.8 (a) Reprinted by permission of *The Wall Street Journal* © Dow Jones & Company, Inc. All rights reserved. (b) All rights reserved; the *San Francisco Examiner;* (c) and *USA Today.*

7.12 Used with permission of *New Management.*

7.13 Used by permission of The Gannett Center for Media Studies, Columbia University, New York.

Chapter 8

8.1 Photograph courtesy of Apple Computers, Inc.; Will Mosgrove, photographer.

8.2, 8.7 Courtesy of Autodesk, Inc.

8.3 (a), **8.8** Photograph courtesy of Broderbund Software; (b) Courtesy of Dominique de Bardonneche Berglund.

8.5 Dial-a-bond infographic. Used with permission of *USA Today.*

8.6 Used with permission of Howard Rheingold.

8.9 © Pixar.

8.10 (a, b, c, d) Computer-modified photographs courtesy of Bob Malecki of Island Graphics Corporation. Reproduced with permission.

8.11 Photography by Marty Sohl. Courtesy of San Francisco Ballet.

8.12 (a) © A. Michael Noll 1965. (b) © Rykmuseum-Kröller-Müller.

Names Index

Subject Index

Spatiality, 44–47
Square, 42
Stenciling, 170
Storyboards, 104–105
Strobe, 169
Sublimation, 3
Superego, 3
Supergraphics, 151
Surrealism, 37
Symbol
  defined, 27–29
Symbols
  knowledge and interpretation of, 40

Television
  and film, 99
  and radio, 97
  as "wasteland," 111
  commercials, 103–108
  genres, 102–111
  image, 97–99
  models for analysis of, 111
  news, 106, 108

talking heads on, 101, 102
  voyeurism and, 99
Television commercials. *See* television
Triangle, 42
Type
  impact of, 138–141
  kinds of faces, 130–138
  size of, 130
Typefaces, 129
  bold, 131, 134
  condensed, 138
  display, 130
  expanded, 138
  italic, 134, 135
  light, 131
  Old English or gothic, 131
  roman, 131
  sans serif, 130, 131
  serif, 130
  text, 130
Typography
  as art, 129
  defined, 129

Unconscious, 2
Unity of design, 144

Vector, 47
Video artists, 110
Video Cassette Recorder (VCR), 101
Vision, persistence of, 18
Visual communication
  decoding, 41
  elements of, 25–60
Visual humor
  allusions, 124
  caricature, 121–123
  exaggeration, 121
  in cartoons, 121–124
  mistakes, 122
  puns, 124
Volume, 43

Watergate Hearings, 101

Z-axis, 53, 100, 101